THE BOAT PLAYS

by

Gil Vicente

Translated and Adapted by

David Johnston

*This book is dedicated to the
memory of Edward Curran*

First published in 1997 by Oberon Books Limited,
incorporating Absolute Classics, 521 Caledonian Road,
London, N7 9RH. Tel: 0171 607 3637 / Fax: 0171 607 3629

author of
ance with

Cover design: Andrzej Klimowski and Richard Doust

Printed by Arrowhead Books Ltd, Reading

ISBN 0 948230 80 0

CONTENTS

INTRODUCTION

Medieval Images Spitting in the Wind

I who lie this stone below
For the Day of Judgement wait,
From life's weary fevered state
Resting now.

(O gram huizo esperando,
Jaço aqui nesta morada;
Também da vida cansada
Descansando.)

Gil Vicente's Epitaph

Any Portugese person asked who Gil Vicente was would reply
unhesitatingly, "the founding father of national theatre in Portugal."
Press them further and the versions would vary. Most would refer to
Gil Vicente as a royal goldsmith and Master of the Mint, but many
would be at a loss to go far beyond popular conjecture. Most of
Vicente's personal biography remains shrouded in mystery. As so
often with Vicente's own characters, it is only against the backdrop
of his work, his social milieu and the payments he was awarded, that
a figure called Gil Vicente begins to acquire a third dimension.
Critical consensus has come to accept that he was probably born
c. 1460-5 in rural northern Portugal which he left, probably in 1490,
to work as a goldsmith to Queen Leonor at the court of João II.
Thus his successful theatrical career began with a highly successful
day-time job as royal goldsmith. His most famous work in this
capacity was the Belém monstrace, wrought in 1506 from the gold
which Vasco Gama transported back to Lisbon on his newly
"discovered" sea route from the East. Vicente's dramatic debut in
1502 with *Monólogo do Vacqueiro (The Herdsman's Monologue,* in
which the ever-willing author took the title role himself) inaugurated
this second incarnation as a dramatist. Vicente was to fashion the
farces, monologues and moralities which entertained and edified
courtiers, returning discoverers among them, at the splendid court
of João II's successor, Manuel I or Manuel the Fortunate.

Compared to many "national" dramatists Gil Vicente was,
for the most part, fortunate too. He made magnificent art from
oriental plunder at the same time as he condemned to hell the moral

climate of greed and usury in which the plundering took place, an ambiguity which typifies the creative tensions often to be found underlying his deceptively simple dramas. A similar ambiguity emerges when his own social position is subjected to scrutiny. In the urban world of court and capital, Gil Vicente, the provincial craftsman, was something of an outsider. Goldsmiths represented a fairly new and growing artisan class whose use to the aristocracy was clearly dictated by the amount of gold pouring into the country. By the reign of João II, a previously embattled Portuguese monarchy was effectively absolute and its itinerant court was a centripetal attraction to any member of the nobility who wanted to get anywhere. As an artisan at the royal court and a member of the "third estate", Vicente was displaced from his humble origins but unusually well-placed to judge the different social strata forming around him. He could observe all the more acutely because neither he nor his profession had any obvious pre-ordained position in the new cross-weave of classes which encircled the omnipotent king.

Gil Vicente was a country boy who made very good indeed. He married twice and was the father of five children. His position as court playwright was to depend, for most of his working life, on the powerful patronage of João II's wife and later widow, the dowager Queen Leonor. From 1508-36 scarcely a royal birth, marriage or death ocurred without finding comment or commemoration in a dramatic tribute from the pen of Gil Vicente. He continued to enjoy royal support even after the death of the dowager Queen in 1525. He received at least one small pension from João III and died in 1537, shortly after the production of his last play in 1536. His collected works were first published in 1562 by his son Luís, in a *Copilação*, under the patronage of João III's widow, Queen Catarina, who vigorously defended his plays from the newly awakened wrath of the Portuguese Inquisition.

Gil Vicente was a court dramatist first and last. One unequivocally positive result of this was his bilingualism. He wrote in both Spanish and Portuguese, sometimes combining both in the same drama as well as incorporating vulgar Beira dialect and bad jokes in Latin in order to construct verisimilitude in the speech of characters from different backgrounds and regions. The *Autos das Barcas (The Boat Plays)*, however, provide a fine example of the juxtaposition of the two vernaculars in different plays with different messages. *Inferno (Hell)* and *Purgatório* are set in Portuguese while the somewhat abstract, formulaic *Glória (Heaven)* was written in Spanish. Vicente wrote for a bilingual court in which Spanish language and letters were held in very high regard. Since the consoli-

dation of Portuguese independence from Castile in 1386, Portugal's
ruling house of Avis had evolved into an absolute monarchy
primarily by curbing the power of a pro-Spanish aristocracy in
Portugal which had fought primarily on the Castilian side in 1386.
In the 15th and 16th centuries the Porgtuguese monarchy adopted
the somewhat double-edged strategy of interdynastic marriage
between the royal houses of Spain and Portugal. This policy reached
its peak in Gil Vicente's time with Manuel I who ambitiously sought
to unite the two Iberian kingdoms under the crown of Portugal by
marriage to Isabel, the daughter of the Catholic monarchs of Spain.
A total of four Spanish Queens, María, Leonor, Isabel and Catarina
coincided with Vicente's incumbency as royal playwright. All of
these Queens supported him to varying degrees. Vicente's easy
adoption of both languages represents a historical high point in
cultural and linguistic symbiosis between Spain and Portugal, at
least at the level of court drama and poetry. Vicente's Spanish was
certainly learned not native. Historians differ as to where he
acquired it. Salamancan dramatists, such as Juan del Encina, were
certainly a significant influence on his work. His natural and
unproblematic command of the two different languages allowed him
to express different but complementary facets of his genius. Just as
much of his dramatic work puts on record the golden period of
Manueline monarchy before decline set in under João III, his
bilingualism exemplifies an optimistic belief in "cultural iberianism"
which the Spanish usurpation of Portugal (1580-1640) was to alter
radically and for good.

In this, as in many respects, Gil Vicente unwittingly stood
at a crossroads. His plays took the right snapshots at the right time.
He had a gift for distilling an essence from the past as it reached the
point of evaporation. In the *Autos das Barcas*, a newly dead cross
section of society make their last journey to "that bourne from
which no traveller returns" only to find their past lives really *do* flash
before their eyes, defined in essence by a Devil and an Angel who
compete for their souls. These plays symbolise better than any the
sense in which Vicente is the dramatist of transition and crossing.
Gil Vicente worked across social classes, across languages, across a
range of professions and, as we will see later, across dramatically
changing time cycles in history. In the *Autos das Barcas* the two-
dimensional drama of medieval liturgy and pageant is stretched out
to encompass an increasingly three-dimensional world. He puts the
old world of Europe on record as it crosses the threshold of the new.
He shows the last attempts of Catholic orthodoxy to reform from
within before the Reformation, the Schism and the final divide. He

fashions the higher points of medieval liturgy, pageant, farce and mummery into a network of social interrelations which enabled Lope de Vega, and later possibly Molière, to develop comedy into a new art. He brings country superstition and the rough dialects of his native Beira to a court that is forced to understand as well as mock a provincial peasantry it usually prefers to ignore. All of these crossings tell us something about the worlds Vicente inhabited and the contacts he forged between them. But what about "our world"? How can this "dramatist of death", so thoroughly defined as a son of the 16th century, make a meaningful crossing into our secular 20th century field of vision, where "carpe diem" remains vivid but the roar of hellfire has become a joke?

I shall attempt to answer this question by consciously avoiding, as *The Boat Plays* wisely do, any obvious, universalist recourse to a clichéd Grim Reaper in a long black dressing gown waiting to pounce from behind the door. Rather, I will argue for Vicente's durability in terms of the contextually specific social satire which one might most have expected to date him. Vicente is a man for our times precisely *because* he was so perceptive a man of his own. He defines, in essence, a concept of non-exploitative social responsibility as the *sine qua non* of salvation from hellfire. His social responsibility retains a powerful resonance for our post-holocaust, postmodern turn of the century where new religions and new humanisms combine to combat our terror of a torment inflicted by man in this life not God in the next. The individual psyche of classical tragedy, the existential anguish of lone man against the universe, the Aristotelian unities of time, place and action did nothing for Gil Vicente's relationship with the dramatic muse. The imperative of Man's "interconnectedness" with his fellow man, not his introspective individuality, is the message which turns Vicente into a transcendent *tour de force* who is still worth paying to listen to. In his allegorical reconstruction of death as the final crossing of the waters, he reminds us, one hundred years ahead of John Donne, that "no man is an island, entire of itself: every man is a piece of the continent, a part of the main;... Any man's death diminishes me because I am involved in mankind, and therefore never send to know for whom the bell tolls; it tolls for thee". Vicente's simple belief in the value of good deeds and altruism foresaw in embryo some of those concepts we struggle to preserve in the 20th century, by enshrining them as human rights. He lived through those earth shattering events which revisionist history, particularly in the wake of the 1992 celebrations, has come to regard as humanity's worst catalogue of human wrongs. How does his perspective on his own times make Vicente so pertinent a prophet for ours?

Although his plays often appear to reflect an immutable
feudal rigidity, Vicente's world was irrevocably on the move in the
great age of maritime expansion. Brazil, the last of Portugal's great
landfalls, had been "discovered" in 1500, only seventeen years before
the first of the *Autos das Barcas* was produced. Vicente's overt
references to the realities of "discovery" are few but the glittering
world which gave birth to his dramas was entirely the product of the
reign of Portugal's *roi soleil*, Manuel I. The Manueline period saw the
early golden days of discovery, the mapping of a eurocentric universe
and the opening of Lisbon and thence Portugal as a porthole onto
the expanding world. The Portuguese papal embassy of 1514
brought Pope Leo X oriental treasures which included the stuffed
body of the first rhinoceros seen in Europe, the posthumous model
for Albrecht Dürer's famous engraving. However, as Vicente was
writing the *Autos das Barcas*, the first thrill of Manueline wonder was
beginning to give way to the worst excesses of exploitative
xenophobia, corruption and vice. João III succeeded Manuel I in
1521. The first serious threats of intra-European colonial rivalry
began to appear on the horizon in an attempt to carve up the
conquistadorial action. The dream of new world wealth enriching
Portugal beyond all imagination was beginning to recede before the
reality of Dutch and British economic preeminence. A century of
dominating the spice route to the East, the richest trade in the world
at that time, left Portugal poorer than she was when she began. How
far did these world-changing events, the consequences of which still
mould our daily existence, impinge on Gil Vicente's dramatic
imagination as he watched from a distance, and listened to the
hearsay, from the comfort of Lisbon, Almeirim and Évora? Certainly,
the ships of the colonial exiles who set forth to the unknown on a
single ticket, find an echo in Gil Vicente's embarcations to
immortality. Vicente makes the point explicitly as Marta Gil, the
market woman in *Purgatório*, fears the devil might be a sailor
rounding up exiles for Brazil, a more immediate threat than hell
itself. However, Vicente's very use of the term *barcas* to describe the
boats of heaven, hell and purgatory dates and delimits his maritime
perspective. The *barcas* evoke the earlier, comparatively "short haul"
voyages which Henry the Navigator sent to Cape Bojador in Africa at
the beginning of the 15th century. By the mid-15th century the
barcas were to become inextricably connected with the superior
marine technology of the *caravelas* and *naus* which facilitated
precision navigation and effective naval warfare. The decline of the
barca symbolises a transition from Medieval maritime adventure to

hard-nosed Renaissance commerce. Vicente's worldview inevitably reflects the circumscription of his life within a closed and specifically politicised court environment and his own mobility was dictated largely by the movements of a peripatetic court. The tall tales of travellers could not have been more than anecdotal evidence in the metaphysical courtrooms where Vicente put the human soul on trial. What we *do* observe, time and again in the *Autos das Barcas*, is the condemnation of a gold lust which Vicente takes care to locate not in the addictive allure of the shining substance *per se* but in the avaricious alchemy of human nature on the make. He exposes not so much the plunder of the burgeoning empire overseas but the feudal exploitaiton of the poor, the fools and the peasantry at home. Each individual soul is answerable for itself but the heirarchy of the system conceals the sinners' awareness of their sins. The royalty and the clerics, unlike the peasants, cannot begin to construct a defence. The higher the character is placed, the greater their certainty of salvation and the greater their horror when this expectation is reversed. In short, Vicente makes a very direct correlation between levels of wealth and status and a propensity to serious sin.

The 15th and 16th centuries probably witnessed more debate that any other period in history as to the nature of the human soul and its capacity for salvation in the non-Christian peoples. 1492 saw not only the legendary arrival of Columbus in the New World, but also the expulsion of the Jews from Spain. The initial tolerance of Jewish refugees in Portugal gave way to restriction of their freedom of public worship in 1497, to their torture and massacre and eventually to their expulsion from Portugal itself. Thus 1492 marked the beginning of the anti-Semitic persecution cycle which was ultimately to drive Iberian Jewry from the peninsula in the wave of diaspora which swept the Sephardics into Eastern Europe. The Inquisition was set up in Portugal in 1536, to test the faith of *Novos Cristãos* (New Christians), usually forcibly converted Jews and Muslims. The 16th century unleashed new and unparalleled opportunities for inhumanity and greed. By 1573, Portuguese royalty was watching the *auto da fé*, the public incineration of live Jews and Muslims, for a Saturday night's entertainment that was comparable with Gil Vicente's theatre. A key issue for the present translator/adaptor must have been the decision to exclude from *The Boat Plays* the Jew who appears in Vicente's *Purgatório* carrying on his back a goat (the scapegoat of the *Book of Leviticus*) which represents the sins of humanity. Even the Devil will not take the Jew on his ship to hell and so the Jew is towed behind, the very lowest and most irredeemable of all the humanity presented by Vicente. As we enter the year that commemorates the liberation of Auschwitz, it is clear that no historical contextualisation of Vicente in his intellectual and religious climate could really erase our sense of horror at this, initially rhetorical, anti-semitism that was soon to give way, under Torquemada, to events that defied representation on the stage. Apologists for Vicente attribute this scene, perhaps justifiably, to his unflinching, journalistic commitment simply to reflect all strata of society and all shades of public opinion, exactly as he found them. In this case we would owe him a debt of historical gratitude for putting it on record like it was. Nonetheless, his treatment of the Jew strikes a jarring note of discord compared with his lyrical compassion for the farmer in *Purgatório* and for the dead child and the fool in *Inferno*.

The 16th century brought Christianity internal as well as external threats of plurality as Europe was rocked by the alternating tides of Reformation and Counter-Reformation. In 1520 Martin Luther burned the papal bull which denounced his writings. Erasmus of Rotterdam was a significant contemporary of Vicente's whose words often find an uncannily direct echo in the playwright's more reformist pronouncements. Much scholarly debate has been devoted to how far Gil Vicente actually espouses heterodoxy by criticising the clergy in *Glória* and whether first-hand Erasmian influence can be detected in the powerful anti-clericalism that pervades much of his work. Critics tend ultimately to find against direct Erasmian influence. Gil Vicente was such an original. He didn't seem to read anybody *very* much. Common knowledge and the local grapevine were as likely to fuel Vicente's critique of Church practices as a trip to the library. His explicit anti-clerical attacks in the *Autos das Barcas* extend to all ranks of holiness and heinousness, ranging from lechery and debauchery among humble country friars, to greed and ambition in the cardinal who aspired to Papal glory, culminating in the wordliness, corruption and simony of the Pope himself. Vicente's *Barcas* certainly sailed fairly close to the wind on this occasion but his broader moral message, "good deeds above all else", was an uncontroversial commonplace in its context. During and before Vicente's lifetime, a growing voice of opposition within Roman Catholicism was objecting to precisely those areas of clerical abuse which Vicente enumerates. No new forms of "sedition" found expression in Gil Vicente. Our clearest indication to the relative impact of his anticlericalism is the fact that all three of the *Autos das Barcas* were left unscathed by Inquisition censorship where other fiercer satires of Vicente's were not. King Manuel himself sent a reformist envoy to Pope Alexander II urging review of the more scandalous disparities between Catholic doctrine and practice. In addition to expressing his own beliefs, Vicente may have used his drama to publicise opportune vindications of King Manuel I's stance. Far more surprising in the *Autos das Barcas* is Vicente's decision to criticise the King himself. It was certainly Gil Vicente's attack on the King, far more than his anti-clerical truisms, which necessitated the improbable salvation of the miserable, high-ranking sinners clinging to the oars that represent the redeeming wounds of Christ.

The *Auto da Barca da Glória* contains the only overt criticism of royalty in the whole of Gil Vicente's *oeuvre*. It is consequently all the more frustrating to the viewer/reader that the King and his "cronies" get off on a technicality at the end of the play. This finally leads me to ask how far Gil Vicente's obvious dependency on royal patronage and his expedient need to please public opinion blur the focus of his satire and compromise the power of his moral message? Analogous issues of popular taste and social acceptability face the current, indeed any, translator/adaptor of the work. Vicente was certainly an astute and multi-talented survivor, who usually knew exactly how to walk the thin line between the satirical caricature which expressed his vision of society and the official dramatic portraiture which "paid the rent". He knew how to inscribe, often quite minutely, the economics and dynamics of the society in which he moved without compromising his survival within the strictures that society imposed upon him. Since many of his court dramas were also subsequently performed in public playhouses in the city it was important for Vicente to reflect current opinion and popular taste without necessarily allying himself too closely with any one position. In this public role, Vicente's caricatures performed a function not dissimilar to our contemporary *Spitting Images* puppets. It is difficult to level any specific objection at *Spitting Images* because all sectors of society are, at least theoretically, legitimate targets of attack. Even the aging Queen Mother, who was initially, if playfully, treated as the ultimate taboo by the *Spitting Images* team, has been added to the repertoire of royalty who are, incidentally, characterised on screen by the props they carry (i.e. Princess Margaret's gin bottle) just as Vicente's figures on stage are defined by their ploughs and work tools. Gil Vicente's grotesque images, however, are more constrained to test the prevailing wind direction before they spit. This renders all the more surprising Vicente's portrayal, alongside the hellbound Pope and Cardinal in *Glória*, of the King whose vision of heaven is obscured by "la muy pecadora vida", "the very sinful life" he has led. Gil Vicente undoubtedly took a chance on this one. He clearly got away with it as he remained in favour with King Manuel I until his death two years later in 1521. Vicente appeared to have

enjoyed the trust and favour of the royal family to such an extent that
the occasional, moral incision that ran too close to the bone was
tolerated in the manner of a carnivalesque safety valve or the sane
and balancing insights of the court jester or fool. Literary posterity
has not always been kind to Gil Vicente's obvious refusal to shoot
himself in the foot. In *The Boat Plays*, David Johnston redresses this
by choosing to replace Vicente's King Manuel I in *Glória* with the
addition of the *Introit* and the *mise-en scène* of the dying Queen Maria,
for whom the *Auto da Barca do Inferno* was tactfully written in 1517.
By his metatheatrical inclusion of the political climate in which
Vicente was constrained to operate, David Johnston effects a
powerful dramatic defence of Vicente's decision to go for the safe
ending. After all, Vicente was not attempting to preach social reform
or revolution. He would not have known what that meant. Nowhere
in his work does he reveal a will to change the system through
revolution or reform. As J. Tomáz Ferreira in the Europa-América
edition of the *Autos das Barcas*, points out, the bourgeois merchant
class who *were* eventually to topple feudalism present a significant
blindspot in Vicente's social panorama. Vicente predates the belief
that the monarchic system could be changed. For this reason, the
Devil's attack on the Queen in Johnston's *The Boat Plays* must
remain resolutely personal, not political. The Queen's "Judge me and
you judge Portugal" is the reflex defence of herself as the "body
politic" which Gil Vicente's audience could have shouted out
unprompted. A sixteenth-century Devil can do no more than
counter, "my Lady, your heart was yours alone". Vicente was
undoubtedly an enlightened man, but he wrote more than two
hundred years before the Enlightenment. Consequently, the
emotional drive shaft of *The Boat Plays*, like that of the *Autos das
Barcas*, is firmly situated in the abuse of the helpless. Vicente's
"lavrador" says, "Nós somos vida das gentes/e morte de nossas
vidas" ("we are the life force of the wealthy/and the death of
ourselves"). In *The Boat Plays* Joane the fool died "alone lying under
a bridge, chilled to the bone, as the city's good Christians walked on
past", the young Prince who burned and battered his child wife,
engages in "the torturing of the weak for pleasure" and the Farmer
whose child dies of starvation is "one whose life was unjust, who
worked like a dog for his honest crust". As David Johnston reminds
us in the Programme Note, "*The Boat Plays* are fired by an elemental
political sense". At Vicente's specific moment in history, this cannot
be a sense of politics, it can *only* be "an elemental political sense". It
informs Vicente's original under two principle guises. In the first
instance, as we have noted, individuals are made aware of their social

responsibility to their fellows. Secondly, we are presented with the concept of a heirarchy of sin whereby the person in power has a greater ethical responsibility to his fellows. This latter view finds powerful support in the common interpretation that Vicente attributes greater blame to the royalty and clergy in *Glória* precisely because the second coming of Christ is required for their redemption. Both of these concepts are central to David Johnston's exposition of the "elemental political sense" underlying the dynamics of Vicentine satire.

The Boat Plays bear interesting comparison, in this respect, with another tradition of Vicentine reconstruction carried out by Northeastern Brazilian dramatists and poets of the 1940s and 50s. Ariano Suassuna (*Auto da Compadecida*) and João Cabral de Melo Neto (*Morte e Vida Severina. Auto de Natal Pernambucano – Severine Death and Life. A Pernambucan Nativity Play*). Northeastern Brazil is the poorest and most drought-ridden part of the country with the vestiges of a feudal system still exploiting the landless poor. In their drama and dramatic verse, Suassuna and João Cabral explicitly rework medieval *autos* such as Vicente's to show "elemental political sense" making individuals aware of their responsibility to each other, constructing a heirarchy of sin which demands a greater ethical awareness on the part of those in power. The true dynamic potential of Vicente's rudimental "political sense" becomes apparent in the context of Northeastern Brazil in the 1950s and 60s. Liberation theology-based grass roots movements made individuals aware of their fellows' suffering and the sense of community they shared. Marxist-led reforms of Catholicism transformed Vicente's concept of individual sin and conscience into the belief that an entire system or a political régime could fall into a state of sin that was collective. Thus we witness Vicente's hierarchy of sin being converted into the sin of "hierarchy" and the "elemental political sense" of the *Autos das Barcas* takes on an active third dimension. By presenting the 20th century audience/reader with that latent vision in Gil Vicente's "politics" which lay waiting for time and tide to release it, David Johnston forces us to ask ourselves all over again what the basic elements of our own "political sense" amount to? He also reminds us why such a question matters.

Hilary Owen

University of Manchester

TRANSLATOR'S NOTE

What first attracted me to *The Boat Plays* is their extraordinary sense of ritual. Of course, any religious ritual, even one as peppered with earthy wit, appears merely arbitrary, emotionally distant from us, if we cannot penetrate to the core of its deeper meaning, what it has to say about the way human beings perceive their place in the divine scheme of things. To read and understand *The Divine Comedy*, for example, requires from many of us today both a suspension of religious disbelief and an abandonment of modernity. In this way, we have to accept *The Boat Plays* on their own terms. They are clearly a wonderfully wrought window into the past, worthy of any intricate Manueline stone-carving. But that doesn't mean that they should excite only a theatrical voyeurism or a scholar's curiosity about late medieval systems of belief. Gil Vicente's words and characters are in one way simply cyphers he uses to depict the procession of souls along the ledge of life and death, balanced between damnation and forgiveness. They are theology made vivid, like a medieval altarpiece. But *The Boat Plays* also communicate the human hopes and fears, the beauty and the terror, underlying that theology. Gil Vicente's voice, with his characteristically quirky tone and his dramatist's taste for the grotesque, comes at us rom deep down and long ago, exploring the shadows that surround the bare facts of our life and death.

In other words, *The Boat Plays* are also theatre of an extraordinarily compelling nature. Such theatre is a journey towards otherness, an abandonment of self. Those decisions I took in order to adapt that sense of theatre for the English-speaking stage as the millenium is about to turn were all geared to drawing out the theatrical experience upon which Gil bases his ritual. Most specifically, all of the characters are explicitly 'written forward' in a way which brings out the whirlpool of dramatic action around which their life has turned. Moreover, Gil Vicente is himself incorporated into this version, not as a fashionable homage to metatheatre, but to pose the central questions which enable us today to grasp theatrically the issues which preoccupied the Portuguese Court at the beginning of the sixteenth-century.

One such question is the relationship between the way we live our lives and the kind of world we live in. For if theology was celebrated as the 'queen of sciences', then politics was the court over which that queen held sway. *The Boat Plays* are fired by a vivid political sense. Like a Renaissance cathedral, they present the sum total of all the relationships that go to make up life in a particular society, in this case the gold-fevered world of a Portugal dazzled by the Discoveries. Gil Vicente wrote these pieces to remind the Court of its ethical and political responsibilities under the implacable eye of God. To abandon such responsibilities, he warns his contemporaries, is to turn the order of creation into the disorder of the grotesque. Such a warning speaks no less to our contemporary experience.

David Johnston

Belfast: July 1996

NOTE: This translation was first performed at the Gate Theatre, London, from 1st to 25th December 1995, and 3rd to 7th January 1996. The production was directed by David Farr and designed by Angela Davies.

INTROIT

The year is 1517. The Jeronomite Monastery on the banks of the River Tagus, on the outskirts of Lisbon. In the chambers of the most Catholic and Holy Queen Dona Maria, the Royal Court has gathered to celebrate the anniversary of the signing of the Treaty of Tordesillas. It is early evening and the reddening reflection of the sun warms the blue-tiled walls. Seascapes through the west-facing windows. A long table groaning with food and drink. Hogs heads and baskets of fruit; pitchers of wine. Around it are gathered, in their gay plumery, various nobles of the court. At the head of the table sits the dying Queen, dressed in white. She is fragile and pale and appears to be asleep. Opposite her sits a man dressed in black, watching her keenly. The name of this character does not appear in the cast list.

NOBLEMAN 1:   *(amidst a burst of laughter)* And then there was this Spaniard *(looking rapidly towards the Queen)*... saving your gracious presence, Your Majesty... this Spaniard, whose humours were so tormented by a predilection for the ladies...

NOBLEMAN 2:   For other men's wives... that, as he himself used to say, he never knew whether he was coming or going... *(daringly)* Saving your sleeping presence, Your Majesty.

NOBLEMAN 1:   That he quite lost his mind. His brain pan dried over and he went off to join the Knights Templar.

NOBLEMAN 2:   So he gave up his nightly pursuits for other knightly pursuits.

NOBLEMAN 1:   The last anyone saw of him, he was storming a castle in Galicia. Alone.

NOBLEMAN 3:   Strange goings on in the neighbouring kingdom of Castile.

LADY 1:   God save and protect us from such excesses.

NOBLEMAN 1:   Pissrogues the Spanish. Mad as gulls.

NOBLEMAN 3:   An inbred people. Their sign is the sign of earth.

LADY 2:   What was the name of the general who went to
                the New World?

NOBLEMAN 2:   Admiral. Columbus.

LADY 2:   He was Portuguese, wasn't he? From Oporto.

LADY 1:   Then why did he sail under the Spanish flag?

NOBLEMAN 1:   They had a whole army sitting on their doorstep
                in Granada, with nothing to do but grow bored.
                Dangerous thing, a bored army.

NOBLEMAN 3:   So send them off on some fool's errand. The
                Catholic Monarchs had no faith in it. Just get the
                army off their backs for a while. Maybe bring a
                few coffers of gold home.

NOBLEMAN 1:   Did I ever tell you about the hermit I met once
                when I was travelling near Toledo? He swore that
                he'd once been a duke, as wealthy as Midas himself.
                And if the truth were told, as much of an ass...

                        The Queen stirs.

LADY 1:   Dom Benito!

NOBLEMAN 1:   ... And what then is Portugal's sign, dom
                Enriques?

NOBLEMAN 3:   Water and air. Sea and sky.

NOBLEMAN 2:   It is the sea that is Portugal's strength. We look
                out towards the new.

NOBLEMAN 3:   And the new will be ours. We shall bring it home.

                The Queen appears to fall back into sleep.

LADY 1:   Perfumes, richer than all the scents of Araby.

LADY 2:   Slaves. As black as night.

NOBLEMAN 2:   And gold. More gold than your mad hermit ever
                 dreamed he had.

NOBLEMAN 1:   There is a city there, in the New World, guarded
                 by eagles and serpents. I heard about when I was
                 in Castile... Potosí... the city is called Potosí. And
                 its riches are legendary. Bare-breasted women,
                 who lie with any man, fountains that flow with
                 wine, gold and diamonds waiting to be plucked
                 like fruit from trees, slaves to bathe you, to dress
                 you... to carry you wherever you want to go. Such
                 things shall be ours as well.

NOBLEMAN 3:   We are on the threshold of the future. The world
                 is ours.

LADY 1:   How did he lose his money? The Duke.

NOBLEMAN 1:   The hermit? He didn't even have a hole in the ground
                 to drop dead in. Never did have. Just mad dreams.

LADY 2:   How grand that sounds... the threshold of the future.

                 *The Queen speaks without any apparent
                 movement. Her voice is thin and querulous.*

QUEEN: We shall not see the future.

                 Clichéd consternation.

QUEEN: But our beloved Portugal is strong and healthy.
                 Our death has no significance.

                 *Clichéd denials. The Queen lapses back into sleep.
                 Silence. Nobleman 3 beckons forward a servant to
                 fill their glasses.*

NOBLEMAN 3:   A health to Her Majesty, Dona Maria, and to the
                 Portugal that she has made great in her image.
                 Long may we prosper together.

                 They all stand, except the man in black.

ALL: Dona Maria and Portugal.

NOBLEMAN 2:   The sun shall never set on this empire of sky and sea.

ALL: To this empire of sky and sea.

NOBLEMAN 1:   You will not drink with us, dom Gil?

NOBLEMAN 3:   Nor even stand for your Queen and country?

LADY 1:   It's intolerable.

NOBLEMAN 2:   A calculated insult.

LADY 2:   Perhaps he's asleep.

NOBLEMAN 2:   Or too drunk to stand.

                 *Dom Gil rises slowly to his feet. His gaze imposes
                 silence. They begin to sit down in disarray.*

GIL VICENTE: *(as though to himself)* You eat like pigs; you drink
                 like sponges; and you speak like fools. *(to the
                 others)* I have listened to your idle chunter all
                 evening. Now I shall speak...

NOBLEMAN 2:   What did you say?

LADY 1:   Just who do you think you are?

GIL VICENTE: I am Gil Vicente. I speak as I write, and in this
                 court we speak as equals.Or do we not? *(silence)* I
                 shall speak, and perhaps you will do me the
                 honour of listening. *(he holds the stage)* Perhaps
                 you will permit me to remind you why we are

here? Twenty-three years ago, on this very
evening, the two most powerful men on earth met,
the Kings of Castile and Portugal, like Caesars
with a sword to split the world asunder, a line on a
chart and all that exists under the sun was
apportioned to Castile and to Portugal. The spoils
of God's creation are divided; wars cease and we
traffick instead in gold, in perfumes, in slaves, in
the unimaginable wealth of the fabled land of Vera
Cruz. The world is ours I have heard you say, and
I pray to God that it is. But I have also had to
listen to the monsters engendered by this
Portugal's fevered imaginations, to delusions of
power. You speak of a history about to be born, as
if there were any history other than the unfolding
of God's plan. Beware, I beg you, of blind angels,
misled by greed, lost in sinful pride, for God's
blind angels shall fall. Creation is not ours to own.

Nobleman 3 strikes the table.

NOBLEMAN 3:   Dom Gil, we have all read your little poems of
                cunning and easy virtue. You think you are
                somehow privileged to lecture us on the evils of...

GIL VICENTE: I am privileged because I see. I write and I speak
                of what I see. Evil is all around us. It is not an
                abstract principle. It is not simply the secular
                meaning we lightly ascribe to gold and the
                madnesses that gold infects. Money is the root of
                all evil, we say, as if money were the simple cause
                of it all... No, evil is present in our hearts,
                'maldade', a force that has been with us since
                creation was ours to touch, a force that harnesses
                our lives, that absorbs our will to the good. I warn
                you because I fear for your souls. Forgive me if I
                offend you, it is not my desire. But I will not
                praise Caesar and ignore God, and I will not
                encourage the passing happiness of men only for
                them to die for ever. Listen to me well, I beg you.
                Your pride and appetites, your greed and your

lusts, your reveries of Potosí, are the work of an
evil which will drive you into hellfire, into a
torment the like of which your straining
imaginations may never even approximate to.
Think of a burning needle in the tenderest part of
your eye, and multiply that pain a thousand times
thousand, and you still shall have no sense of...

NOBLEMAN 1: Frankly, such bitter sentiments in the presence of
her majesty, whom you know not to be enjoying
the best...

GIL VICENTE: I speak of this because of my gracious Queen, for
whom I have nothing but the tenderest of loves.
(turning towards her) My Queen, your death will
not be insignificant. Death is the doorway to truth.

NOBLEMAN 2: Truth is what you live. The truth of life. Of
Portugal and of the New World. Of man and God
in harmony.

GIL VICENTE: And you call Spaniards pissrogues, as mad as gulls!
You laugh at madmen, at the poor wretch who
thinks himself a duke! Life is an easy dream. What
will any of us die as? What will God make of your
soul when you finally wake? Or of yours? Or yours?

NOBLEMAN 3: And of yours, good dom Gil?

GIL VICENTE: Or of mine.

LADY 1: Look, really, I think this is in very poor taste.
Considering...

GIL VICENTE: Considering we all shall die, whether in gentle old
age or with the life suddenly forced from our
shocked lips and bursting eyes... Man builds up
treasure here and today feels immortal... but I tell
the youngest of you in this room, the pine trees
from which your coffins will be cut have already
been felled, and their wood is already curing.

NOBLEMAN 2:   *(with a nervous laugh)* So carpe diem, what...?

GIL VICENTE: Beware the day. Beware the evil of which we are part.

LADY 2:   Are you saying we are all condemned to hell?
                What have we done to deserve such horror?

NOBLEMAN 3:   And Her Majesty?

                *The Queen suddenly puts both hands on the table
                and addresses Gil Vicente directly.*

QUEEN: We thank you, Gil Vicente, for your concern. Our
                priorities are clear. We shall hear no more talk of this.

GIL VICENTE: What else should we properly talk about? My duty...

NOBLEMAN 3:   Sir, you verge on insolence.

GIL VICENTE: Sir, the truth cannot be insolent!

                *The Queen's head once again slides forward,
                although her hands remain on the table. Her voice
                is a distant murmur.*

QUEEN: Tomorrow, dom Gil, tomorrow. Tell us your
                truth tomorrow.

GIL VICENTE: I shall bring the devil himself here tomorrow. I
                shall parade all life before your eyes and I shall
                state the vigorous accusation that the Enemies
                make against all men when their souls abandon
                their mortal bodies.

NOBLEMAN 3:   Words, dom Gil, words. Each man knows his soul.

GIL VICENTE: Ah, you think so. I think I shall show you
                differently. Show. Not tell you. I shall arrange a
                performance that will reveal to you the truth. And in
                order to show you, I shall create an expanse of sea, a
                river so wide no eyes can cross it, so deep no stone

can plumb its depths, and each soul that arrives at
that desolate shore shall find three boats, one that
goes to heaven, one to purgatory, one to hell. And
you shall participate in my playacting perhaps as
unknowingly as you participate in your own.

QUEEN: We are tired. Tomorrow morning, you shall come
                  to my chamber with your players. There the court
                  shall gather while we breakfast. Then perhaps we
                  shall see. But tonight we have other things on
                  which to think. You may go, dom Gil, since you
                  clearly find this company distasteful.

GIL VICENTE: With your leave, my gracious queen. I must
                  prepare. My only concern...

                  *Words fail him. He stands, bows stiffly and leaves
                  in silence.*

NOBLEMAN 1:   A Christian gentleman. What is it they say about
                  dom Gil? A man so truly humble that he feigns
                  arrogance... he would hate anyone to applaud his
                  Christian virtue.

                  A loud burst of laughter.

THE BOAT TO HELL

*The chamber of Queen Maria. Bright morning light through latticed
windows. The shadow of a boat. The court in audience. Silence as Gil Vicente
takes his seat. A figure explodes from nowhere, dressed as a boatman.*

DEVIL: The boat, the boat, my friends, this is the boat.
                    All on board for hell, for I've taken note
                    of everything in life that you have been;
                    there's nothing that you've done that's not been seen,
                    your loves, your lust, your pleasures, even dreams,
                    they all have their price, all their hidden seams
                    of guilt and sin for the Devil to mine.
                    The diamonds and rubies of shame and crime,
                    laying treasures in store that corrupt us
                    so that when life's done and the coitus interruptus,
                    when some unseen hand plucks you from your bed
                    or when in the street you fall down dead,
                    you'll find yourself here in my boat so grand,
                    crossing with me to the island of the damned.
                    The benches are clear, the tackle tightened,
                    we're ready to sail with souls enlightened,
                    finally, horribly awake at last;
                    now there's no turning back, the die is cast.
                    Life's passed through your hands like water on clay.
                    Put it any way you want, you've had your day.
                    And since we're all the children of our acts,
                    it's time to face the music, pay the tax.

NOBLEMAN 1:   Hello! You! Good man.
                    Tell me where I am.

DEVIL: Handsome, dom Benito, you don't know me?

NOBLEMAN 1:   You, a fisherman?

DEVIL: Is that all you see?
                    Look into your soul, look into my eyes...

NOBLEMAN 1:   Then a ferryman...

DEVIL: Who demands his prize.

NOBLEMAN 1:   Where is your boat bound?

DEVIL: We leave with the tide.

NOBLEMAN 1:   Where?

DEVIL: You know where!

NOBLEMAN 1:   Where?

DEVIL: Just get inside!

NOBLEMAN 1:   Sir, once and for all,
                where does this boat call?

DEVIL: Sir, once and for all, listen to me well.
                You are dead and this boat is bound for hell.

NOBLEMAN 1:   So hardly a cruise,
                no bracing sea breeze.

DEVIL: Handsome dom Benito laughs death in the face.
                Sir, you mock even in this dark place?

NOBLEMAN 1:   You know who I am?

DEVIL: I know who you were.

NOBLEMAN 1:   My soul's in safe hands,
                in my wife's good care.

DEVIL: Will she pray for you?

NOBLEMAN 1:   She'll always pray!

DEVIL: Crave indulgences, a mass said today...

NOBLEMAN 1:   Pardons bought tomorrow.
                Thus time is borrowed.
                My soul gains its rest,
                in heaven with the best;
                a cushion of faith,
                so push on off,

mate. In the naval sense.

DEVIL: Handsome dom Benito,
Damascus has no perfumes or scents
powerful enough to cleanse your soul's stench.
Your father once sat here; now it's your bench.

NOBLEMAN 1:   Is that how he went?

DEVIL: They all go that way.
What you sowed back there, you reap today.

NOBLEMAN 1:   Give me time, I pray.

DEVIL: You are freight for me.

NOBLEMAN 1:   Look another boat,
he'll sort this out.

DEVIL: You are freight for me.

NOBLEMAN 1:   Boatman, you, kind sir.

DEVIL: You are freight for me.

NOBLEMAN 1:   Help one who is blind, sir.
Who admits his sin.
What a mess I'm in!
Ahoy there, mate... sir.

ANGEL: A little late, sir, don't you think? You're dead.
There's still time to repent on one's last bed,
not when you're waiting on this stony shore.

NOBLEMAN 1:   Where do you sail for?
Kingdom come or hellfire,
paradise or pit?

ANGEL: I sail to God's port,
to rapture, to bliss.

NOBLEMAN 1:   Transport to transport!
Then I'll pay my way. I'm landed gentry.

ANGEL: A tyrant!

NOBLEMAN 1:   You can't refuse me entry.

ANGEL: Camels and needle eyes... you know the story?

NOBLEMAN 1:   Why is it so wrong?

ANGEL: Why is it so wrong
                to abuse your power, to lie, to beat, to whip?
                Such airs and graces would sink this small ship.

NOBLEMAN 1:   I demand respect.
                I'm owed it. I expect
                red carpet treatment,
                not this debasement.

ANGEL: You snap your fingers, others have to jump.
                That's your sin, your flaw, that's your camel's hump.
                You despised lesser folk, looked down on them,
                and as you grew prouder, became less than them.
                You will sail to hell on the next high tide
                in a boat whose size will match your pride,
                so your grandeur, airs and finery all fit,
                a cargo of sin to take to the pit.

DEVIL   *(singing)* The sea is like glass.
                Little fish glide by.
                The sea is a mirror.
                To see your life pass by.
                Dom Benito, look with me into the deep.
                Watch yourself die as you lie in your sleep.

NOBLEMAN 1:   Oh, that other life,
                and my darling wife,
                tears flowing like water
                for my departure.

DEVIL: Though not the tears that'll save you from hell.
                Remember, people cry with joy as well.

NOBLEMAN 1:   None was loved so well!

DEVIL: You haven't seen the half.
                    While you were in your bed, growing cold and stiff,
                    she was with her lover, growing warm and stiff,
                    screwing, fucking, having it away,
                    isn't that what you mortals like to say?
                    Look into the water, you'll see her mouth
                    a name not yours, then cry out in love
                    just as your soul flees with your last breath,
                    your lips blue and cold, the stertor of death.
                    Watch her lips open and close in pleasure,
                    as yours close for ever; a memory to treasure
                    for eternity.

NOBLEMAN 1:   Then let's go on board.
                    I thought I was adored.
                    I believed the lies.
                    Oh, God how time flies.
                    Yesterday, power;
                    today the final hour.
                    This boat is burning
                    and there's no turning
                    back.

                    This last word echoes emptily. A Moneylender
                    arrives carrying a bag of money.

DEVIL: Manuel Dos Santos, I know you so well.
                    I've reserved your seat on the boat to hell.
                    Accept my congratulations, Satan knows,
                    on the nobility of your death throes;
                    Oh such courage, what brave demeanour!
                    Only very rarely have I seen a
                    death of such quality, of such gentle bliss...

MONEYLENDER: Who the hell do you think you are?
                    Me fresh dead and you taking the piss.
                    Let me tell you, chum, life was sweet
                    and I would have stayed longer
                    if I'd had any say in it.

DEVIL: My friend, death is always stronger.
                    Between life and death there's no truce;
                    life goes on, like a whore plies her trade,

but when death calls, then there's no use
crying, weeping, pleading for more.
What's in your bag?

MONEYLENDER: A bit of food.
For the journey.

DEVIL: How very nice.
Not that it'll do you much good
where you're going.

MONEYLENDER: Do I know you?

DEVIL: Manuel, I am you and you me.
Think: that night thirty years ago,
that dark night when you first knew me.

MONEYLENDER   *(his voice an echo in time)*
There is no God. There's just money.
I'll make a life of silver and gold;
Satan, give me credit to start.
There's not a soul can't be bought and sold.

DEVIL: The night you sold your soul to me.
You don't need to be reminded.

MONEYLENDER: Look, dom... whatever your name is...
You're overly literal minded.
They were words, just meaningless words.
Lovers promise undying love;
the guardians of the truth all lie;
we all swear faith in God above.
What more can I say? Empty words!

DEVIL: What if we call it a contract?
You're a man lived inside the law,
who used its fine words to extract
every pound, every last penny.
Yes, words can lie, and do usually.
On this seashore let's be honest
– what you did was plain usury.

MONEYLENDER: The law is law and words are words.

By law, I'm a merchant banker
who deals in futures, stocks and shares...

DEVIL: Morally, sir, you are a wanker!
You were Satan's little helper,
and such a very greedy one,
lending to the poor and hopeless,
each of the city's needy ones
was another profit for you.
What's in your bag?

MONEYLENDER: Nothing for you.
There's another boat over there.
Hey boatman, lucky I saw you,
I'm on my way to paradise
and I want to charter your boat.

ANGEL: You've got money?

MONEYLENDER: I've a fortune.

He pulls notes galore from his bag.

ANGEL: With such weight, we'd not stay afloat.

MONEYLENDER: I've much more at home in a chest,
ten million, take me back for that
and we'll both live off the interest.

ANGEL: You've a contract with my fallen friend.
It's a lot more than my job's worth.
Talk to him.

The Angel turns his back on the moneylender.

MONEYLENDER   *(to the Devil)* Take me to heaven,
and I'll make it more than well worth
your while... I'll throw a million in,
two million more when we arrive.

DEVIL: The devil's easily tempted,
but not three, I'll take you for five.

MONEYLENDER: Five million's all I've brought with me.

DEVIL: I knew that all the time.

MONEYLENDER: All right.
                 (I'll undo the deal when we land)

                 He hands the bag to the Devil, who ushers him on
                 board. As he climbs the gangway, the Devil
                 empties the bag into the sea. It is full of nothing
                 but gaudy paper scraps.

DEVIL: You'll sup with God this very night.

MONEYLENDER: Remember we have a contract,
                 for which you have been royally paid.

DEVIL: Such generosity of soul
                 will produce its own rich reward.

                 The Moneylender settles into the boat.

                 Your faith in me is touchingly absurd.
                 After all, what's a contract but your word?
                 And what's a word in one who's lived like you
                 but a hollow mockery of what's true.

                 Meanwhile on the boat.

MONEYLENDER: Dom Benito! What a happy chance!
                 You have a small debt outstanding...

NOBLEMAN 1:   You may collect it when you wish,
                 for all its use.

MONEYLENDER: Upon landing.
                 There'll be use for it in paradise.

NOBLEMAN 1:   In paradise, good dom Manuel?
                 You think you've bought your way to God?
                 This very night we'll burn in hell!

DEVIL: You'd do better to save your breath to row.

The tide's running high. It's nearly time to go.

A Fool arrives.

JOANE:	Hello! Yoohoo!
DEVIL:	So who are you?
JOANE:	It's me. Just me.
DEVIL:	Just you. I see.
JOANE:	Can I come on?
DEVIL:	Of course, you can. When did you die?
JOANE:	I'm dead, am I? Yes, I fell sick... it was over quick
DEVIL:	This fool shouldn't be here for a week yet. Still, if I can lure him into my net... though I do wish he'd speak in longer lines, it's such a strain to think of the rhymes.
JOANE:	I was on my own... I died alone.
DEVIL:	You're here too soon!
JOANE:	I died at noon.
DEVIL:	It's only nine!
JOANE:	I can't tell the time.
DEVIL:	Imagine eternity spent with him, his vacant gaze and his toothless grin. What death brought you here?
JOANE:	I've no idea. The runs and shits

yes, that was it...
I've had them bad
since I was a lad.

DEVIL: I'll enjoy his companions' reaction,
with his bowels in constant liquid action.

JOANE: Where's it go, this tub?

DEVIL: To Beelzebub.

JOANE: Beelzebub! Old Nick!
I'm getting off! Quick!

> *He pauses to take breath. Then like a single
> exhalation.*

Off you go on your cuckold's boat,
blubber lip, yokel woodcutter,
worse than a lawyer from Lisbon,
with your scabby wife
spawning frogs
and your grandsons full of shit.
Your father steals onions
and you've been excommunicated,
booted out like a donkey,
a cuckolded donkey to boot.
Your wife's a rat
and there's shit on your sail,
you blubbering and bragging
leg of an old grasshopper.
They cut off your balls in Braga
and your tail caught fire in Faro.

> *He pauses, panting, then notices the other boat.*

I've told him what's what.

ANGEL: Yes, I noticed that.

JOANE: Are you the devil?

ANGEL: No. I'm his rival.

JOANE: My name's Joane.

ANGEL: In that case, come on.
                Simple Joane, I watched you die alone,
                lying under a bridge, chilled to the bone,
                as the city's good Christians walked on past
                you called out for help, then gave up the ghost.
                They think a down and out doesn't feel a thing,
                anyway, they don't owe you a living,
                so they let you die in the cold and rain,
                another hopeless case gone down the drain.
                Give me your hand now. Come into the warm.

                The Angel helps Joane into the Boat to Heaven.

JOANE: A hand? Have an arm!

                *A Friar appears, holding a girl in one hand and a
                shield and sword in the other. His tonsured skull
                glistens under his sweaty cap. He is dancing with
                the girl.*

DEVIL: Good Father, holy Jesuit...

FRIAR: I don't think I've had the pleasure...

DEVIL: You've had more than enough of it,
                I'd say. So you enjoy dancing,
                you and your sweet little companion.

FRIAR: I see you find her entrancing.

DEVIL: Is she yours?

FRIAR: I bring her as mine.

DEVIL: What did your brothers say to that?

FRIAR: She was out of sight, out of mind.

DEVIL: A girl who's slept with a friar,
                where do you think she should be sent,
                to sit with God or burn in fire.

FRIAR: I'm not into theology,
            I'm more a social sort of priest...
            but if...

DEVIL: Enough codology!
            That first night you lay in her bed,
            when she confused God's love and yours,
            that night you joined the eternal dead,
            that night when she put her arms round you,
            when she confused God's love and yours,
            you lost God and the Devil found you.

FRIAR: Holy body of sweet Jesus.
            Does this habit count for nothing?
            My love for you?

DEVIL: Your love teases
            the flesh.

FRIAR: I am weak.

DEVIL: You are lost.

FRIAR: Am I so easily condemned?
            All my life I've embraced the cross.

DEVIL: All your life you've embraced warm flesh.
            You chose to waken the serpent,
            and you've danced to the serpent's hiss.
            Your fumblings and prayers in the dark,
            'I know you're troubled, my daughter,
            let me bring peace to your sore heart.
            I'm a man of God, and I care.
            I beg you, please put your faith in him,
            while you're at it, put your hand down there'.
            And you remember how she let
            you take her and take her again?

FRIAR: Remember? Will I ever forget?
            I'm to be damned for that love?

DEVIL: Sex,
            let's call spades spades, shovels shovels.

FRIAR: A question of Christian ethics?
            By St Ignatius, I'll debate those!

DEVIL: You fool, you understand nothing.
            You don't see what's under your nose.
            But the lust under your habit
            moves you like the dog wags its tail
            and the fox chases the rabbit.
            You see nothing but what you feel,
            and you feel only between your legs.
            For you the only thing that's real
            is what you can have, take or steal.
            I condemn you in Satan's name.
            Your sentence has now been decreed.

FRIAR: Sweet Jesus, when I took my vows
            this was not what you and I agreed.
            All the prayers, the hymns and psalms...
            Oh, God help me... God's angel there,
            divine boatman, have you no qualms
            seeing my soul in this distress?

            The Angel turns his back. Joane looks up.

JOANE: Pretty mistress,
            wouldn't you rather
            some how's your father
            with a saintly drunk,
            not an evil monk?
            One Good Friday
            he confessed me.
            Father I have sinned
            he told me to begin.
            Sinner you have fathered
            I should have said to him.
            Father, get to hell.

DEVIL: So reverend father, you've heard the sentence
            out of the mouths of babes and innocents.

            A well-known madam , Brizida Vaz, appears.

DEVIL: Ah but, father, before you go,

before you climb on board my boat,
here's somebody I'm sure you know,
somebody who's procured for you
and who in turning up like this
has finally secured for you
your place in hell's conflagration.
Now, I wonder what happy chance
brings about this assignation.

BRIZIDA: I told you I'd see you in hell
when your knife plunged into my breast;
and by Satan it serves you well
that you should rot for killing me.

FRIAR: You murdered me with your poison;
hemlock in my wine filling me
with the fear of God and of death.
You were blackmailing me, vile whore!
You were robbing me of the breath
of honour and reputation.

DEVIL: Brizida, you must put your case
tell us why you've earned salvation.

BRIZIDA: I have suffered such vile torments,
so many whippings, such abuse,
at the hands of lustful clients
that like Christ, scourged and stripped,
my soul stands naked before you.
Why must such a pure heart be shipped
off to hell, with this sinful crew?
Hello angel, hello lovey,
anything I can do for you?
Looking for a bit of business?
You look lonely standing up there,
fancy a voyage through the senses?

ANGEL: You were well paid for your whipping,
with your cupboard full of lashes;
I'm afraid your style is slipping,
Brizida Vaz. What's in your bag?

BRIZIDA: Six hundred false hymens

– only the finest ladies buy them.
so they can be virgins again.
All sorts of things to please men;
three trunks of secret potions,
powders and pastes. Oh, and some lotions
for itchiness and sores,
the sort you get from whores.
What else? Bats' wings, sheeps' eyes, a vixen's melt.
Look a master key for a chastity belt!
Silk cushions to lay on the floor,
lies and intrigues... by the score.

ANGEL: Each of these items has its cost,
but they are not your real cargo.
Your real cargo are the souls you lost,
of the girls you sold like cattle;
each time a girl gave herself for you
we heard her soul's death rattle.
That's your cargo.

BRIZIDA: I'll tell you more,
my pretty boy, listen to me;
Yes, I provided girls by the score
not just to little guns like him,
but to canons of the Holy See.
I've served the church in my own way:
apostle, angel and martyr,
with many works of charity.
Should such a saint have to barter?

DEVIL: Tell us more of your divine acts.

BRIZIDA: A thousand women came to me
to make their maidenheads intact
after...

ANGEL: After?

BRIZIDA: Riding horses,
those nasty little accidents.
I simply restored their losses,
repaired them with needle and thread
to avoid unholy discord

that first night in the marital bed.
I swear to you Saint Ursula
converted less maidens than me.

ANGEL: I tell you this: that poor fool there
            did more for his fellows than you.

DEVIL: Brizida, come on board my boat.
            Victim and executioner,
            sooner or later most men are both.
            Sit between the priest that cut you up,
            and the girl you sold for pleasure,
            who died, drinking wine from his cup.

            A Judge appears.

DEVIL: Welcome, my learned friend! A man of note
            and wisdom, please step on board my boat;
            a Queen's Counsel, a Judge, who took silk
            but kept an iron fist; I know your ilk.

JUDGE: Speak only when you're spoken to!
            Right! First things first, just who are you?

DEVIL: *(he speaks in the voice of an old woman)*
            I stole the bread.
            We hadn't eaten for three days or more.

JUDGE: *(unwillingly)* Bread's still property.
            Not eating's no defence under the law.
            You are guilty
            but too old to be imprisoned and tortured.
            Your sentence is this:
            you shall be hung and your body quartered.
            Take her down.

DEVIL: *(in the voice of a frightened child)*
            Sorry, your worship
            I promise I won't throw stones at priests again.

JUDGE: *(unwillingly)* Priests are pillars
            of life; they mediate between God and man.
            You have offended

against the known laws of all creation.
You'll be taken out
and sent to the constable for flagellation.
Take him away.

DEVIL: Let's be clear; I'm full of admiration
for one so removed from the temptation
to cloud judgment with the milk of kindness.
You dispensed the law and dispensed with justice.

JUDGE: But you shall not decide where I am taken.

DEVIL: I take the souls that God has forsaken,
and your soul is destitute and vacant
like the bed of a prostitute in lent.

JUDGE: Videtis qui petatis? Super jure majestatis.

DEVIL: You can vade retro with your Latin.
To be a judge you only need a smattering,
enough to terrify the innocents
and put a gloss on legal nonsense.

JUDGE: All my life I defended law and order.
These are the basic principles for there
is no property or gain without them.

DEVIL: And if the hungry steal bread, then clout them,
torture them, hang, draw and quarter them.
You became a judge for the common good,
or to protect the interests of your brood?

JUDGE: I shall not listen to these cheap jibes.

DEVIL: One small point: nonne acceptistis bribes?
I hope the Latin minimises the shock
of suddenly finding yourself in the dock.
But it's not the favours and corruption
that have led to your final destruction,
not the self-interest and over-weaning pride
but your support for a world where love died,
designed to exclude the dispossessed, the poor;
that hate will keep you from heaven's door.

A Lawyer appears just at this moment.

LAWYER: Judge Carvalho, I kiss your bounteous hands.

JUDGE: Learned counsel, you here in these sad lands!

LAWYER: Who is this boatman? What is he saying?

DEVIL: That you'll both be good for rowing... and flaying
           alive.

LAWYER: Is this your idea of a jest?

DEVIL: Your friend isn't laughing.

JUDGE: I think it best
           we listen to him.

LAWYER: What's his angle?
           I'm a lawyer. If he wants to tangle
           I'll take him for every last escudo.

DEVIL: It really doesn't matter what you do,
           it really doesn't matter what you say,
           this is one judge that can't be bought or swayed.

LAWYER: *(spotting the Angel)*
           You threatened to pressgang and batter us
           in front of a witness who'll stand up for us.
           Sir, I call upon you to testify,
           for this boatman's wild threats should horrify
           every right-thinking person among us.

JOANE: I'm left thinking –
           too much deft drinking
           Men of learning,
           quit your guerning;
           You lived off cheating,
           and stand there bleating
           like lambs of God.
           Bugger off to hell.

ANGEL: Good doctors, let me carry out my function

in this trial. Did you receive extreme unction?

LAWYER: I'm a doctor of laws, not a medic.
               How was I to know my illness was chronic?

ANGEL: In that case you didn't prepare your brief
               because it's life and not death that's the thief,
               life that clouds our gaze to infinity
               and blinds our hearts to iniquity.

JUDGE: I made a good last confession, I'm sure.

ANGEL: Hiding nothing from your confessor?

LAWYER: Don't answer that. It's a leading question.

DEVIL: I was there, and I made a suggestion,
               a word in your ear as you confessed.
               All those bribes, the favours, it would be best
               not to mention all those backhanders,
               for if I don't return them they'll land us
               in trouble. No absolution for me.
               Think back: that voice. That resolution to be
               dishonest, even to the bitter end.
               That's what's brought you to this, my stupid friend.
               You're no sooner up than down, on life's wheel.
               Now get on board.

LAWYER: We'll get him on appeal.

BRIZIDA: Here's the judge who made my life hell on earth.
               How many times he asked me "What's it worth
               to stay out of jail?"'. I was always giving.
               After all, a girl's got to make a living.

DEVIL: All on board, my greedy and lustful crew.
               It's been a pleasure doing business with you.

               A Hanged Man appears.

               Well, well. Room for one more inside.

HANGED MAN: Take pity on poor Barrabas!

DEVIL: But Barrabas lived, it was Christ died.
You died for someone else to live.
I find such selfless abnegation –
from an infernal point of view –
a horror and execration.

HANGED MAN: Garcia Moniz had said to me...

DEVIL: You moved in exalted circles,
the President of the Treasury...

HANGED MAN: ...that those who chose to die like me,
who lay down their lives for others,
died in the odour of sanctity.

DEVIL: Put like that, it sounds very nice.

HANGED MAN: He said it was proven that God
loves those who make such sacrifice,
that I was the chosen of the Lord,
that the judges knew of the sham,
that he, Moniz, had given the word.
Tomorrow you'll sup milk and honey,
in paradise, he promised me,
and your family'll have the money
to buy the things that make life sweet.

DEVIL: What is it people say... that life's a bitch?
The poor make their living dying for the rich.

HANGED MAN: In that final step, he whispered to me
that here was the place of the elect,
where the rope hung from the lemon tree.

DEVIL: Did this bring you consolation?

HANGED MAN: The noose was snug around my neck,
all I felt was trepidation.
You can afford to feel devout
if you're going back home to the wife;
the sermon's harder to swallow
if it's you that's losing your life.

DEVIL: Did he speak to you of purgatory?

HANGED MAN: He spoke of the prayers for the dead
sung at the mass of Saint Gregory,
that he would pay for the mass
and say a hundred novenas
so that my soul would quickly pass
into the kingdom of the blest.

DEVIL: I don't know what to make of this,
you've clearly died before your time,
your name isn't on my lists.
I'm afraid that makes you a suicide.
I'll check with goody two shoes there.
What do you think?

ANGEL: I coincide
with everything that you have said.
His body lies in unhallowed ground.
As far as we're concerned, his soul is dead.

> *The Angel of the Lord turns his back on the
> Hanged Man.*

DEVIL: So you see, that's the way of it.
The cosmic joke's at your expense,
You die, and it's you who'll pay for it
with eternal torment in hell.

Get on board, the tide's high, it's time to go.
Right, my dead friends, it's time to start to row.
We go to the place where there's no tomorrow,
but eternal darkness and black sorrow,
where your suffering will as endless be
as night without day, as the boundless sea.

> *Four Knights of the Order of Christ come in,
> having just died in parts of Africa. They sing the
> following song.*

KNIGHTS We died in burning sun.
God's will be done!
We lie buried in African sand.

Tonight we'll sup at God's right hand!
The boat of life is ours by right,
for we have fought God's good fight,
and laid down our lives in sacrifice.

DEVIL: Your words, I'm afraid cut little ice.

KNIGHT 1:   Satan, turn your head as we pass.

KNIGHT 2:   Lucifer, look on us and you will burn.

KNIGHT 3:   Beelzebub, take care who you address.

KNIGHT 4:   Anti-Christ, you will learn
the force of good from this bright swift sword.

ANGEL: Saints without stain, knights of the Lord.
The boat to heaven awaits
your good command.

THE BOAT TO PURGATORY

The same day. The flooding light of noon.

GIL VICENTE: Life is but a dream;
and death the final awakening,
never more to sleep.
Have I shown you enough,
my friends?
I think not,
for you hang on to your compendium of dreams
of power
of riches
of greed
of lust
like drunkards to their last glass.
The sea of the dead is dark
beyond your dreams,
beyond memory,
and those you saw embarked
on the first journey were all lost,
damned to its darkest depths.
The sea must be crossed,
death cannot be obstructed.
You shall all awake,
my friends,
as surely as night follows day.
Prepare yourselves.
Close your eyes,
look into the darkness.

The theatre is gradually reduced to total darkness.

All the landmarks fade;
all the dreams die.
Open your eyes now,
look into the dark
and prepare.
In the midst of light

Light slowly returns.

you are in darkness.
It is Christmas Eve.
In the false light of your false day,
look into that darkness
and in that darkness
you shall find light.

A pealing of bells.

ANGELS   *(singing)* This is the boat to God's glory,
the boat that's bound for his sweet side,
speeding swift and safe for the more we
grow close to God, the more we may thrive.
From the first star to the last grave,
look upon these banners of light
raised high and valiant to save
those whose eyes are dimmed by life's dark night.
The sea tonight glistens like glass,
the tide serene, by winds untorn;
souls, give thanks to God as you pass:
Tonight is our saviour born.

The Boatman from Hell enters.

DEVIL: What's going on here, in the name of Lucifer?
Has every last sinner been reduced to prayer?
Not a soul in sight – never better said:
Come on you sinners, you blind and you dead!
Don't waste your time with candles and psalms,
the tide's ripe for those who lived without qualms.
After all, what's life for but the living?
It's for the taking, not for the giving.
To sacrifice is to live absurdly,
this rich world is only for the worldly.
Enjoy it, then come to me on this ledge
with your burden of dreams and passion's pledge.
This fine boat awaits, newly planed and tarred,
for those whose love is of life, to hell with the Lord.

ANGEL: There is one love and no other,
and on this night you must plead

and pray to our holy mother
with words that weep and bleed.
Of all women she is the rose,
and each of your sins a thorn
but tonight her love for you flows:
tonight her son Jesus is born.

DEVIL: I see I'll have my work cut out tonight.
But some pig with his snout so deep in the shite
that his stench is beyond all washing away,
even this damned night, is bound to come my way.

Enter a Farmer, carrying his plough on his back.

Speak of the devil.

FARMER: The sea already!
Does the sea come so far inland?
I'd only seen it once before,
when as a boy I was pressganged,
and taken off to fight in the war.

DEVIL: I've been waiting for you my friend.
Go on, pitch your plough into the sea,
and stop awhile, rest here with me.

FARMER: I know you, and I know you'd send
me packing off to burn in hell.

DEVIL: You've worked so hard, put down your plough.
Let me wipe the salt sweat from your brow.

FARMER: Damn your eyes, I know you too well,
and I've heard your honeyed words before,
breaking stones in the sun's leaden heat
or cutting trees in blinding sleet:

FARMER AND
   DEVIL: 'Put down your plough. You can do no more'.

FARMER: I've worked for the right to curse you.

DEVIL: That was advice not temptation.
            I've looked inside your imagination,
            I know the secrets you nurse there,
            and if I'd wanted you to feel desire,
            it wouldn't have been with your labour
            but for the blonde wife of your neighbour.
            I'll fetch her now if you accept hellfire.

FARMER: When I died, fear and desire died too.
            I stand before you easy of mind.
            Look back into my life and you'll find
            all in order, all you tried to
            undo has been firmly secured
            and left in its place, where it belongs.

DEVIL: Arrogant fool, what about the wrongs
            you've done, or are you hopelessly inured
            to your own sins, your cupidity?
            This is your boat.

FARMER: This is a farse.
            Come over here and kiss my arse.
            It's the nearest you'll get to me.
            I died a Christian on Christmas Eve.
            You can stuff your cupidity –
            what does that mean? – some stupidity
            of yours, I'm sure. I'll take my leave.
            That's a better boat over there.

ANGEL: Ah, good farmer, I know you too,
            your old self as well as the new.
            You should take your business elsewhere.

FARMER: You'd turn me away just like that,
            one whose lot in life was so unjust,
            who worked like a dog for his honest crust,
            you damn me at the drop of a hat?
            What meaning is there in such a life?

ANGEL: Did you repent at the very end?
            Did you ever seek to make amends

for all the evil, all the strife?

FARMER: The priest said 'Make an inventory
                   of everything you've said and done
                   so that when you're finally dead and gone
                   – for this is what was meant to be –
                   I will assume your soul's beast of burden.
                   All I ask is that you confess
                   and make a donation to redress
                   your most woeful sins. I'll put a word in
                   with God. Your soul will gleam like new.
                   I promise you'. It made sense to me,
                   I paid for ten masses and a litany.
                   I did what the church told me to do.

ANGEL: You believe you've earned eternal rest,
                   that sin's so lightly washed away?

FARMER: I blessed myself and prayed each day,
                   I believed the credo to the last.
                   I did what the church told me to do.

DEVIL: You did what? For whose greater glory?
                   Yours is the same old sinner's story:
                   you only did what was best for you.
                   Shall I proceed with my accusation?

FARMER: What have you got to accuse me of?
                   Why should God refuse me love
                   and condemn me to dark damnation?

DEVIL: You sold diseased stock, you stole water,
                   you moved fences and you took the land...

FARMER: And for that you'd have me damned,
                   you miserable dog? You ought to
                   look into your own diseased heart.

DEVIL: I am disease and I am pride,
                   I am all the sins you carry inside.
                   Look into your own diseased heart.

Think back ten years ago last September,
when you looked up towards the sky
and wept and cursed God on high,
you commended God to hell. Remember.

FARMER: I remember that autumn well;
it rained and rained, day after day;
the field were flooded, crops washed away.
We'd nothing to eat, nothing to sell.
My son was ill, he was only four...
he needed good food, nourishment.

ANGEL: The rains were God's punishment.

FARMER: He died.

DEVIL: A casualty of war,
between God and man put to the test.

FARMER: He died... he was taken from us,
snatched by a God whose promise
of love we had believed.

DEVIL: A jest.
God has a sense of humour... of a sort.

ANGEL: The little one is at God's right hand.

FARMER: Leaving me alone to work the land
and my wife to grieve distraught!
In my anger I cursed God's name
and I raised my fist against the sky.

ANGEL: You called out and God heard your cry
and condemned you to eternal shame.

DEVIL: Looks like I'm on to a winner!

ANGEL: But you shall avoid damnation
on this night of reconciliation,
a truce between God and sinner.

You shall walk on this frozen river day and night,
that you shall cleanse and purge your soul
until time and cold do take their toll
and God has mercy upon your plight.
And you shall not put down your plough
until time itself shall come and go.
You shall pray for God's love in limbo,
and not rest till you hear his word. Leave now.

DEVIL: You're going to let him away with that crap?
All that talk of peace and pacts, of goodwill?
All they want is to erode your freewill,
God's little mouse, a man in a rat-trap.
All this fuss to get into that dump?
Just think of it: the humiliation,
the breast-beating, the self-deprecation.
You've cursed God. Now give his angel a thump.

FARMER: I have no faith in time, less in the church;
my life seemed to fade in a single day;
my punishment will soon pass away.

DEVIL: Unless God just leaves you in the lurch.

            *He leaves. A Market Woman appears. Her name
            is Marta Gil.*

            You can never tell with God.
            He can be, well, odd.
            Ah, Marta, fresh from the market,
            you smell of cabbage and fish.

MARTA: You don't exactly smell of roses;
more kind of brimstone and sulphurish.
How do you know my name anyway?

DEVIL: You're a sight for sore eyes, my pretty rose,
Marta Gil, my lovely Marta Gil,
a treat for the eyes, less so for the nose.
I love the way you swing your hips. Style!
They must have worshipped you on the stalls.

MARTA: Who are you? A sailor? Boatman? A tramp?
          Anyway, you talk a lot of balls.
          You're not in charge of the labour gangs...?
          Look, I didn't mean what I just said.
          I don't want to be exiled to Brazil.

DEVIL: Marta Gil, Marta Gil... you're dead.
          But say the word, and over the night we'll ride:
          take my hand and come on board with me;
          Marta Gil, Marta Gil, my chosen bride.

MARTA: I've heard that voice and those words before,
          a thousand times... I know you so well.

DEVIL: And I saw you born, I've watched all your tricks,
          seen you cheat, always ready to sell
          cat for hare and carp for finest cod.

MARTA: You bastard, that's what you call cheating?
          Far worse things go on in higher places.
          So quit your whingeing, stop your bleating.

DEVIL: They are the deeds by which you are known.
          All the people you left complaining...
          their hard-earned cash and all that food poisoning.
          I find it really quite entertaining.

MARTA: Say what you like, you slimey old shite,
          it's the way of the world, the law of life.
          We all take our profits where we can,
          it won't keep me from the afterlife.
          Who is it that win's people's respect,
          loser or winner, rich or poor?
          I lived and died in a time of greed,
          and there's one thing of which I'm sure:
          a profit must be made, come hell or highwater.
          So give us a break and get off my back,
          if I'd gone and wasted my time on earth,
          then I'd understand why I'm being attacked.
          But I've worked my backside into the ground,
          selling eggs and fruit, meat and fish, and veg...

so what if I made a few pence here and there,
and put aside a bit for my old age.

DEVIL: And all the milk you poured and sold
                that you mixed with water and sour slops?

MARTA: You'd guern away till the cows come home...
                or until somebody like me stops
                you in your miserable tracks.
                Come anywhere near me, I'll break your arms.

DEVIL: Come on board, my sweet and lovely Marta,
                we're all bewitched by your gentle charms.

MARTA: Holy angel, take my basket on board,
                because it's turning my brains to paste.

ANGEL: The basket contains your world of sin,
                a whole planet of greed, a life of waste.
                Would you load such sin onto this fine boat?

MARTA: In life you accept the smooth and the rough;
                it's give and it's take; it's what life's about
                and it's true of the market, and of love.

DEVIL: Now aren't you a good one to talk of love?
                Your heart's as hard as the meat you sold.
                I know you, Marta Gil, inside and out.

ANGEL: Marta, you stand upon the threshold
                between heaven and the fires of hell.
                Think very carefully, then tell me why
                you have any right to come on board here.

MARTA: Because, my Lord, I do not want to die,
                because my whole life has just been work.
                I've never known real love, even friendship.
                I was born to trade in the marketplace.
                Have mercy on my soul, your Lordship!
                I don't want to be locked out of heaven.
                You say I carry a basketful of sin

but am I to be damned for ever
for mirroring the world that I lived in?
Holy Mother, forgive these sad sins
in the name of the child born this night.
Don't leave me lonely on this cold shore,
my lady, don't snatch away my birthright.
I don't understand what my sin is,
I don't understand this accusation.
But I won't go on Satan's boat tonight,
even under pain of excommunication.

ANGEL: Marta, you may yet save yourself through prayer
that will purge your sins on this frozen shore;
but you will feel great pain and grief,
a torment that will eat at your heart's core.
And your pain will be pitiful to behold;
you will burn, you will freeze beyond the scope
of anything that you can imagine.
But this suffering can be your only hope.

MARTA: I shall embrace that suffering as my own;
such pain, such grief, will keep me from damnation.
In my life, I've never stopped to think
or feel; this is my only salvation.
But there is one thing I want to say;
one thing eternally engraved upon my heart;
I didn't know that God's love was so strict.
The market rules should be made clear from the start.

>   *She begins her lonely walk and fades into*
>   *darkness. The sound of the sea.*

DEVIL: Christmas Eve, I'm getting old.
I didn't use to feel the cold.

>   *He sneezes.*

ANGEL: God bless you! A turn of phrase.
It's what Gabriel always says.

>   *The sound of the sea.*

The air's so pure, the sea's glistening
with its specks of blue phosphorous.

DEVIL: Frankly, I would prefer
something a bit more sulphurous.

A Shepherd appears.

Christmas Eve! That's all I need. A shepherd!
If you're looking for a stable, mate,
you're about fifteen centuries too late.

SHEPHERD: Is this a post or pillory or what?
Some sort of gallows?
How many have you hung out here tonight?
Quite a few, I suppose.

DEVIL: You've a black sense of humour, I see.
You like your little jokes.
I'm sure we could share a few here on board.
Could I perhaps coax
you to step this way. Come and see my ship.

SHEPHERD: I'd be well pleased to visit such a vessel.
I've never seen such a thing.

He goes to step on board. A sudden gust of wind.

That wind carries with it the smell of death.
It's some sort of warning.
Who are you?

DEVIL: I am a shepherd of men.
Come and join my flock.
I'll lead you to a place that's green and lush.

SHEPHERD: I'll not get on that crock.
If you're not Lucifer, you're the next worst thing.
And I'm not crazy.
Though I can't remember what I died of,
and my memory's hazy,

but I came here direct to seek the Lord...
that's one thing that's clear.
I came along here without a worry...
Oh yes, you can sneer,
but I know who I am and what I've done.
They buried me today
and my mother's still weeping at the grave.
You'll not take me away
for her tears will lead me straight to God.

DEVIL: How very touching!
Do forgive me if I seem cynical,
but I think you're clutching
at straws. Mind you, you are a drowning man.
My considered impression
is that the only thing you've got going for you
is your profession.
Christmas and shepherds. Spots and leopards.
You'll be mine tonight.

SHEPHERD: And you're a fat rat with stinking death breath.
A bastard and a shite,
with your spider's face and your cockroach eyes...
and you've got leprosy.

DEVIL: These are the ravings of a drowning soul;
pure idiocy.
You're a poor thing, shepherd, but you're mine.

SHEPHERD: Oh, am I indeed?
What can you have to say about my life?
What are my misdeeds?

ANGEL: Shepherd, did you die a good Christian?

SHEPHERD: What a question!
I dirtied myself, I vomited up my food...

DEVIL: I have a suggestion.
A way to prove your Christian credentials.
Say an Ave Maria.

But get it wrong, shepherd, and you are mine.

SHEPHERD: Terrible diarrhoea...
                My bowels were heaving all night long.

DEVIL: All then right, a novena.
                Anything at all to cleanse your soul
                of such misdemeanour.
                No? You don't know any magic words?
                No hocus pocus?
                No mumbo jumbo springs readily to mind?
                All those words that choke us
                and stick in our throat. I know you, my friend.
                Your soul's as black as mine,
                wizened and shrivelled like shite in the sun.
                And still you whine
                and whinge and mutter that you're heavenbound.

ANGEL: Then try the Our Father.

SHEPHERD: Ourfatherwhichart... blessedbythy... em

DEVIL: Perhaps you'd rather
                have a go at the Kyrie Eleison?
                Why don't you, instead,
                just admit you're a miserable sinner?

SHEPHERD: Why don't you drop dead?
                I used to know a lot of the Lord's Prayer
                and the Hail Mary bit.
                How does it go...Hail Mary, holy Mary...
                Once I could say it
                in my sleep, when I was a lot younger.
                My life has been tough,
                I worked day in, day out, like a mule.
                I'd no time for this stuff.

ANGEL: No time to give thanks to the God who made you?

SHEPHERD: I did my work well;
                what better way is there of giving thanks?

I believed in God
but every waking moment was for work;
This is my reward?
I believed in the church, in its doors and roof,
its windows and walls;
I praised God and I ignored the devil,
I ignored all the calls
of the flesh, all of his temptations...

DEVIL: Is that strictly true?
I have a note here: ask him about Esther.
A matter to pursue.

SHEPHERD: Tell me what I did to her that was wrong,
the nature of my sin.
Once we danced all night, I held her close to me...
I felt her silken skin...

DEVIL: You dress up your lust in very fine words,
terribly romantic.
Of course, I'm just an old cynic at heart,
horribly pedantic.
I seem to remember that you intended
to have your evil way;
you boasted to anyone who'd listen
she'd be yours one day;
that you'd have her, by hook or by your crook.

SHEPHERD: So what, she refused,
you bastard son of a pox-ridden bitch,
so why am I accused
if the matter came to no wicked head?
She ran like the wind
and I had no heart to chase after her...
how can I have sinned?

ANGEL: It's not simply a question of the success
of your attentions.
You must know the road to hell is paved
with good – and bad – intentions.
I pity you, but such a soul's not prepared

for God's promised lands...

DEVIL: Don't waste your pity on his blackened soul.
                I'll take him off your hands.

SHEPHERD: How can you damn my soul to living hell
                at holy Christmas?
                Has my life been so dark, so unruly,
                my sin so monstrous?

ANGEL: Listen carefully to what I'm about to say.

DEVIL: 'Listen carefully to what I'm about to say?'
                The correct term is 'hark',
                especially at Christmas to shepherds in the dark.

ANGEL: I shall ferry you to God in all due time,
                but first you must repent
                of a life lived in ignorance of God's law,
                of passion and love misspent.
                Walk this frozen river in fire and in cold
                till I beckon you on board;
                and that time may come when you've learned by heart
                all the praises of the Lord;
                and forgotten the sinful name of Esther.

SHEPHERD: I'll forget my name as well
                if that's what it takes to get me to God,
                and keep me out of hell.

                        He fades into darkness. A Shepherd Girl appears.

GIRL: Help me, oh, help me, please;
                I'm lost; I was dreaming
                I was in dark hades,
                but I can't be; I'm freezing.
                You are the Enemy,
                I saw you in a dream
                or through some alchemy
                or dark unholy scheme.

DEVIL: You saw me when you died;
            as your eyes closed for good
            I was summoned to your side,
            to watch your life conclude.
            Why do you think that should be?

GIRL: I died a girl of twenty.
            I lived as well as could be,
            a life of joy and plenty,

DEVIL: With no thought for tomorrow,
            a life of heedless pleasure;
            and you wonder that this sorrow
            should visit such easy leisure.

GIRL: I thought I would enjoy old age,
            I thought I would live for ever,
            my life was an unwritten page...

DEVIL: My heart bleeds for you. However
            you lived like all young rebels,
            you ignored your God,
            you praised the Devil,
            but you, unfortunately,
            did not live to make amends.
            You died importunately.
            Which is why your presence offends
            and is repugnant to our Lord.
            He's turned his face from you.

GIRL: What have I done wrong? I adored
            my parents and I loved God too.

DEVIL: The gentle goodness you protest
            is as plain as any pikestaff.
            I believe you. I'll do my best
            to intercede on your behalf.
            Come on board with me, my queen,
            and I'll take you to paradise,
            and all that will be, is and has been
            will be laid out before your eyes.

I'll lay creation at your feet,
unroll the world like a chart God sent;
just come on board with me, my sweet;
you shall abide to your heart's content
in the place of eternal prayer,
where your grandparents went before.
Place yourself in my paternal care
and we'll set sail to God's bright shore.

GIRL: Your words are reassuring,
but I saw you as I died
and I felt that you were luring
me to Satan's side,
and as I felt the final pain
and as my mother wiped my face,
I heard you laugh and laugh again
and thought: he thinks that I am his.

DEVIL: I'll make you queen of all you see.
You died a humble shepherdess;
But if you come and lie with me
you'll live an eternal empress.
Anyway, you hardly died a virgin.
One more won't make any difference.

GIRL: And you're no better than vermin
and I resent your inference
that I'm no better than a whore.

DEVIL: The inference is mine, the law is God's;
I saw you with them, by the score,
I saw them all, lucky sods.
I watched you stand before them naked,
not a shade of shame in your heart,
all the secrets of your sordid
little flings, my pretty little tart.

GIRL: Your mind's as twisted as your face,
there's nothing human you understand.
I grew up in a magic place,
I grew up upon my father's land,

a running child in fields of wheat;
I lived among the fruit and flowers,
and felt the earth caress my feet.
and across all those happy hours,
I bathed and swam in mountain streams,
and I gave myself to the summer air,
I lived in my world of dreams
in a world without sin or care.
I grew up under the stars and moon
and I watched the seasons turning,
and I thanked God for this good fortune.

DEVIL: It won't stop you, my love, from burning,
from suffering cruel expiation.

GIRL: The fault's not mine; it's the earth's,
it's the glory of God's creation.

DEVIL: Really? You're making things much worse.

GIRL: I loved the glory in all things,
I gave myself to the beautiful.

DEVIL: So that's the reason for your flings.
Bad mistake. God loves the dutiful,
my daughter; the sensual is mine.
And now your body's in the ground;
that golden skin turns to dust in time,
your flesh breaks up, your bones grind down;
creation and death work hand in glove.

GIRL: I lived with never a thought for death.

DEVIL: Death will be your body's final love;
she's taken you; you've felt her dry breath
as she pressed her mouth down hard.
Sic transit gloria mundi.
The kiss of death; life's a graveyard
where you'll all fall and rot one day;
your destiny's putrefaction;
all else is the lie of one day,

of the most fleeting satisfaction.
Unless...

GIRL: Unless what?

DEVIL: Unless, of course,
you give yourself willingly to me.
The Devil cannot take by force.

GIRL: The Devil will never take me.
Holy Angels, help me I pray!
Get thee behind me, Satan!
Holy Mother of God, this day
deliver me from temptation.

DEVIL: *(urgently)* Beautiful shepherdess,
holy temptress,
listen well;
in hell
I'll give you fields of clover.
Life need not be over,
your flesh need not strip
in the earth's cold grip,
your breasts need not decay,
simply say
you'll come with me
you'll ride with me
across the sea tonight.
Everything you desire,
diamonds and sapphires,
frankincense and myrrh,
you'll find there,
simply say
you'll come with me...

GIRL: Holy Angels, help me I pray!
Get thee behind me, Satan!
Holy Mother of God, this day
deliver me from temptation.

ANGEL: Shepherd girl, leave him and come here.

GIRL: Who are you. I trust no one.

ANGEL: I am God's Angel, have no fear.
I bring tidings of God's holy son.
He too suffered such temptation
and the power of will you have shown
has saved your soul from damnation.

DEVIL: No! She must reap what she has sown.

GIRL: I was too young to know better.

DEVIL: Come with me and I'll say no more.
No? She sinned. God will not let her
sail to heaven from this shore.

GIRL: Angel, take me from this sad place.

ANGEL: You cannot go to heaven yet,
your soul's not ready for God's grace,
but all your sins may be offset
by walking on this God-forsaken shore.

GIRL: How long must I walk in this pain?
How long will it be before
I feel the light on my face again?

ANGEL: Accept the mystery of this frozen place,
remember your sin,
and beg God for his warming grace.

She fades into the darkness. A young boy appears.

BOY: Mama,
it's dark.
I can't see.
Where are you?
Don't be long.

DEVIL: Child,
come here.

BOY: Who are you?
                I don't like you!

DEVIL: You stole
                your brother's penny.

BOY: I didn't.

DEVIL: Come here...
                or I'll bite your hand off.

BOY: Mama.
                He's going to eat me.
                Get papa.

DEVIL: Bah!

BOY: I'll call our Joane!

DEVIL: Bah!

BOY: If he hits you,
                you've had it.

DEVIL: Bah!

BOY: Is that all you say?
                Just bah?

DEVIL: Bugger off.

BOY: I can hear
                my mama crying.

ANGEL: Her grief
                knows no bounds,
                but you belong to us.
                You shall
                always be with us,
                and God
                secretly

does you the greatest mercy
in your age of innocence.
That is the root
of the enigma.

Singing, the Angel places the boy in the boat.

DEVIL:

Enigma? Well, I don't understand.
I know what I see, what's in my hand.
The night's done. I'll get the sail unfurled.
Fuck it. It's a pity about the girl.
I hate going back empty-handed,
she'd've been some catch to have landed.

A song is heard.

I'm a rambler,
I'm a gambler,
I'm a long way from home
and if you don't like me
just leave me alone.
I'll eat when I'm hungry
and I'll drink when I'm dry
and if red wine don't kill me,
I'll live till I die.

DEVIL:

Aha! I recognize that fine song
and I place my trust in this man's wrong
for he's a gambler and a schemer,
a hopeless drunkard and blasphemer.
I have high hopes for this one.

The Gambler appears.

My partner, my very good friend,
walk no further. This is journey's end.

GAMBLER:

Any chance of a drop of wine,
my old son?
I've been walking all bloody night,
and I'm nearly done.

DEVIL: My friend, I'll stake your eternal soul
            on the turn of a card.
            If I lose I'll drop my claims on you,
            you'll sail off to the Lord.

GAMBLER: I've never turned down a wager yet.
            Let me cut the pack.

DEVIL: Now take your card...is it a good one?

GAMBLER: It is. Hearts. The jack.

DEVIL: Now I wonder if I can trump a jack?
            Spades. Of course. The ace.

GAMBLER: Perhaps we can call it double or quits.
            I'll cut... just in case.

DEVIL: Don't you trust me? Anyway I won't bet.
            You've nothing left to lose.

GAMBLER: You can have the souls of my wife and son.

DEVIL: No, they have to choose.
            I can only accept what's freely given.
            What else have you got,
            bearing in mind you're mine, body and soul.
            I think I've got the lot.
            But if you like, we'll roll the dice, one last time.

GAMBLER: I've rolled a seven.

DEVIL: If I roll more, you'll solemnly curse the host.
            Less, you go to heaven.
            A nine! Some call it the magic number.
            And you lose again.

ANGEL: You've turned the host into a thing of sport!

GAMBLER: I'm not to blame.
            'He who blasphemes well believes in God'
            I've heard it said.

ANGEL: You have blasphemed against the holy state.
            You've gambled and you are dead.

GAMBLER: I was caught up in the rules of the game.

ANGEL: Plant born of a bad seed,
            you shall burn in the hottest fires of hell,
            and none shall intercede
            to keep you from the holy wrath of God.

GAMBLER: Luck held me in a spell,
            she was the mistress of my every move.

ANGEL: Luck may incline, not compel.
            No star forced you, It was your inclination.
            Even on this night
            one who sells his soul
            can have no possible salvation.

            *The Devil snatches him and carries him away,
            singing a discordant song. The Boat to Heaven
            sets sail, with the boy on board. The shore remains
            deserted apart from the wind and the occasional
            moving shadow of a soul in torment.*

THE BOAT TO HEAVEN

Evening. Mass is being celebrated in the Chapel of the Queen. Candlelight.
All the members of the Court are present, including the Queen. They sit
stiff and unbending on ceremonial chairs. Gil Vicente kneels. A statue of
Our Lady of Perpetual Succour stands in a corner niche.

GIL VICENTE: *(standing)* The boat to heaven.
                  The final sailing.
                  It is hard to believe in evil,
                  but evil is real;
                  it is in our hearts,
                  it is part of us;
                  and it is hard to believe in death;
                  the death that is ours,
                  but death too is real,
                  and comes marauding out
                  from the heart's silent deep.
                  Your days are as nothing;
                  your power is abandoned
                  your favours withdrawn.
                  All shall be undone
                  within the fire.

                  The Statue of Our Lady fades as the figure of
                  Death appears in another corner of the stage.
                  Death may be played by Gil Vicente.

DEATH: What do you want of me?
                  I'm cold.
                  I have business to attend to.

                  The Devil appears.

DEVIL: Then go about it well.
                  You bring me only the poor,
                  those broken
                  on the wheel of life.

DEATH: Who would you have me bring?
                  I bring the dead,

not the quick.
I serve neither you
nor God.
Death is beyond all good
or evil.

DEVIL: You bring me children,
you bring me minor officials,
you bring me farmers and shepherds,
animals themselves on the land,
you bring fishwives
and whores.
I want the powerful.
I want the Queen.
Bring me the Court of Lisbon,
I want to sink my teeth
into their sin.

DEATH: They conceal themselves well,
better than lizards in sand.

DEVIL: Will you bring them?

DEATH: Their flesh is sweet,
their blood is warm.
I'm so, so cold.
They must pay their debt to me.
How shall I bring them?

DEVIL: A fever.
A diamond from Vera Cruz,
from the land some call Brazil.
A ship docked last week
in Lisbon,
laden with the seeds of death.
Many will die.
Bring me the Court.

ANGEL: Oh Virgin Mary, Our Lady
be their saviour
in this the hour of their death.

Their days are as nothing.

Death returns, bringing the Duke.

DEATH: You, sir, fine and elegant Duke,
            you should know death's your only queen;
            your allegiance has been misspent.

DUKE: I know who I am, what I've been.
            You plucked my soul from my body,
            but I will not recognize your sway.

DEVIL: As soul's go, it's fairly shoddy,
            prone to fierce pride and gluttony...

DUKE: I am a grandee of Portugal,
            a noble...

DEVIL: That's the irony,
            that one so noble and so proud
            should possess a soul so black and mean,
            that such a fine bearing should enshroud
            a spirit so shrivelled and sick.

DUKE: I demand respect!

DEVIL: You demand?
            Your tomb demands respect... phallic
            sword, hounds at your feet, cherubims
            weeping round your head of marble,
            a mourning host of seraphims
            dancing like angels on a pin.
            Your soul's quite a different matter;
            not marble, pus; not glory, sin.

DUKE: That body took this soul to war
            and I earned the right to that sword
            fighting for God and Queen afar;
            such a soul was cut in battle
            and such a soul has won God's favour.

DEVIL: All talk, my friend, empty prattle.
            You killed and enjoyed the killing,
            you boasted of the soldiers slain
            you glorified in the blood spilling.

DUKE: I am heavenbound as surely
            as my stone tomb will last for ever.
            Angels, you know I acted purely
            to create God's empire on earth.
            I fought for civilisation.
            That, sir, is the sum of this soul's worth.
            I saved a thousand Indian souls...
            if souls they may be deemed to have.

ANGEL: They have an animus, like a dog or cat,
            they may never know heaven or hell.
            When the body dies, well, that's that.

DEVIL: Whether or not they have souls,
            they have bodies that bleed and scream
            on the rack or scorched with burning coals.
            Your future lies far out to sea.
            The horizon's a burning bridge
            that tonight you'll cross with me.

            LESSON

DUKE: Lord, your hands made me,
            created and shaped me.
            Tell me then
            why you are so quick to destroy?
            Do not forget
            this clay that suffers.
            You gave me bones,
            sinews and life,
            you breathed your grace
            into my mouth.
            Save me now
            from Satan's grasp.

DEVIL: I have to admit, you do things well.

Your words, your deeds, your loves, your death...
all the strutting of an empty shell.
I shall take you across the bridge.
I've come for you, to claim my own;
tonight you'll take your final voyage.

DUKE: The wound
in sweet Jesus' side,
his passion on the cross,
has redeemed the lost.
I am of his glorious band
and I shall embark
for his eternal land.

ANGEL: The divine laws are founded on good,
equal and proper in all respect.
Mortals may redeem themselves through deeds.
Therefore, Duke, what can you expect?
You have killed, you have corrupted.
There's no place in heaven for you.

DEVIL: Sorry to have interrupted
what was really quite a fine speech,
but the time has come to set sail,
the tide is rising on the beach.

DUKE: The sufferings of Christ were in vain!

ANGEL: Christ suffered for you to argue here.
You have no just cause to complain.
You lived a life entirely free,
you moved and did as you saw fit;
here you must register your plea
that your living was worthy of him.

DEVIL: That's it in a nutshell, good Duke.
That's what it's about. What a shame...
Now get into the boat and row,
for the night and tide are rising quick
and you have a long way to go.

*The Duke boards the Boat to Hell. Death returns
leading a young Prince by the hand.*

And still you bring me children!
Are you frightened of the powerful?
Bring me a king or a statesman,
bring me a pope to dance on his grave.

DEATH: This is no boy, this is no child,
            no innocent God may easily save.
            Look close; he is an infante of Spain,
            a boy of fifteen with a wife of ten,
            a boy who lived to inflict hurt and pain.

DEVIL: Don Rodrigo, welcome to this fine place.

PRINCE: Who are you? I fell off my horse...
            Who are you? I know your face,
            but I can't remember where we met before.

DEVIL: In dreams, my spoilt and sullen little prince,
            in your dreams where you learnt to be so cruel.

ANGEL: He is a child!

DEVIL: He is a husband and a prince!

ANGEL: He did not choose to be so!

DEVIL: Your church made him so!

ANGEL: He is an innocent!

DEVIL: He is a monster of nature
            with evil in his heart.

PRINCE: What have I done that you find so bad?

DEVIL: You tortured a girl barely ten years old.

PRINCE: She was my wife.

ANGEL: In the eyes of man and God.

DEVIL: Not your marriage's sad consummation.
            But the beating and the burning,
            the venting on her of your frustration
            because papa wouldn't give you the white horse.
            You gouged her eyes and you burned her legs.
            Go on, tell us now of your remorse.

ANGEL: Boys are noted for their acts of cruelty.

DEVIL: This isn't like pulling wings off flies.
            This is the abuse of a prince's fealty;
            the torturing of the weak for pleasure.
            I sang in your heart as she begged you to stop.

LESSON

PRINCE: Holy Jesus,
            we are born
            and live
            in blackness.
            Be thou my light
            and lead me now
            to your side
            and to your forgiveness.

RESPONSE

            I have sinned,
            but I sinned
            out of a child's ignorance.

ANGEL: Satan, you shall not take this child from me!

DEVIL: Fool, I'm inside him still. He's mine already!

ANGEL: I see his heart and his heart's crystal pure
            for his repentance is noble and sure.

DEVIL: I move within him like fish in the sea.

I am part of him and he is part of me;
he is a puppet; watch me pull his string.

PRINCE: Telltaletit
             your tongue shall be slit
             and the palace dogs
             fed with it.

DEVIL: Tell us more.

PRINCE: I hated my wife
             and if I'd had a knife
             I would have cut her
             to the bone.
             But papa
             said the throne
             could only be mine
             if I took her
             as my bride.
             He called her bait
             and he explained
             that it was
             a reason of state.
             I want...

DEVIL: You wanted

PRINCE: I wanted to be king

DEVIL: And would have done anything.
             Your malicious plan
             was never that of a boy
             but of a man.
             The boy is long dead
             and the man shall rot in hell.

             Death returns.

DEATH: The fever is running high;
             Lisbon shivers and burns in turn.
             I bring you your highest prize.

> *The Queen appears. As she does so, both the*
> *Queen and courtiers in the court audience stiffen*
> *visibly. For a moment it seems they will interrupt*
> *the performance.*

DEVIL:

Your Majesty! This is an honour.
I shall accomodate you well.
At long last! The Queen a goner!
A bit of the quality trade,
here's history in the making.
This way, Your Highness, don't be afraid.

QUEEN:

I fear no one nor anything.
Judge me and you judge Portugal!
Not even Satan dares such a thing!

DEVIL:

My Lady, your heart was yours alone;
you reigned over a time of greed;
your public image set the tone
for a nation embarked on madness;
for a nation which has lost its way.
And in your heart there is badness,
for we are the childen of our acts.
Though you professed reasons of state,
it's time that we faced the silent facts,
not the facts history will relate,
the discovery of new worlds,
the wealth that's made Portugal... great,
but a private story of pride,
of overbearing arrogance,
a cold heart that scorned and despised
both rich and poor, the weak and strong.
You were adored but made no good
of allegiance, of the great throng
of people who professed you love.
You remained apart, aloof,
you lived in a world above
the ordinary stuff of life;
so that when your soldiers killed and maimed,
when the madness for gold ran rife
in your name, you felt no concern.

Your heart was frozen and closed
to things that made decent stomachs churn.

LESSON

QUEEN:

My soul is weary
of a lifetime of suffering,
and the sins I lived
preclude the glory
my soul desires.
In bitterness,
I speak out
these most painful of words.
Of my soul
I shall speak to my Lord,
saying
with pitiful tears:
Do not condemn me,
but show me why
you allow no one to save me.
I am yours;
I was your regent on earth,
but if I fall to hellfire
then whose shall I be?

ANGEL:

Heaven is of such heightened glory
the soul must be of purest gold.

DEVIL:

My Queen, your soul is of iron;
as hard as iron and as cold.

RESPONSE

QUEEN:

Lord, highest Lord,
I beg you
do not remember my sins
in final judgement,
when you destroy this world
in your fury of fire.
Bring me to you now,
by the right path.

Let me appear
in your presence.
Sweet Jesus,
they burdened
you with the cross
for all sinners;
you were beaten for us
and taken to death.
Pray for us now
and take our fears away.

DEVIL: A crown of thorns suits you well,
your words, your tone, very sincere...

Pause. Suddenly in a frenzy of fury, to the Angel.

She has fallen from grace!
This exercise in face
doesn't fool me.
She is guilty
of abomination,
of adulation
of gods of power.
In one short hour
she'll not be reborn.
She was warned.
Her spirit was depraved,
by Lucifer she'll not be saved!

Lamely.

Over my dead body anyway.

To the Queen.

We'll sail on the next high tide.
There's the boat. Now get inside.

Death returns.

DEVIL: Ah, my good friend, grey and hoary,

trailing your clouds so gory,
who's next for my consideration?
I love a good humiliation.

DEATH: The whole city's panicking,
they're falling like flies in winter.
Death takes them like a hurricane
in autumn lifts up a dry leaf;
the whole city weeps like a child,
echoing with cries of pain and grief.

DEVIL: It sounds prodigious beyond measure;
your words bring a glow to my heart.
Now who's next for my displeasure?

DEATH: The Emperor of Holy Rome,
no less.

DEVIL: With or without his Empress?

DEATH: Without.

DEVIL: I used to watch her comb
her hair, long and liquid and black,
with such an intense perfume...
She was a nymphomaniac.
I wonder if he knew that...

DEATH: Don't you know for sure already?

DEVIL: I can make myself forget what
knowledge and memories I choose;
I deny myself omniscience,
as God does, so as not to lose
interest in the dramas that unfold
in front of me on this cold shore.

The Emperor enters. He is clearly in distress.

Prosperous Emperor, fine lord,
I trust your journey has been unpleasant.

I bid you welcome on board.
You clearly had no conception
of the age of living's painful close.
It's our immaculate deception.

EMPEROR: My death was painful and obscene,
I have no wish to suffer more.

DEVIL: On the other hand, your living was clean,
a life of luxury and ease.
The time has come to pay the price,
for here all debts...

EMPEROR: I beg you, please,
I have suffered a lifetime's pain
in the horror of these last days.
If I were to have my life again,
my only thought would be for death.
The splendour, power and glory,
an empty sham and shibboleth.
My crown of plumes and gold and silk
is undone before my enemy,
the fine robes in which I clothed my guilt
are now torn and shredded rags.

DEVIL: Your Glorious Majesty,
you must forgive me if my mouth sags
open comically at your words,
at such humble protestations,
the most convincing that I've heard
for a couple of centuries now.
The endless cruelty, violence,
the mindless whims, all this you disavow?

EMPEROR: You were an angel and you fell,
you fell senseless from the sky
and you drag others into hell
to accompany your lonely torment.

DEVIL: Your theology is faulty,
even in its rudiment.

I did not fall; I was pushed!

LESSON

EMPEROR: Who will help me
              and protect me in hell?
              My humanity is weak
              and I cannot hide
              from your anger
              and righteousness.
              Lord, make your terror swift,
              pass over my guilt.
              I am a sinner,
              yet I shall answer
              with my turbulent soul.

RESPONSE

              Oh, free me, Lord
              from eternal death
              and everlasting condemnation.
              Raise me
              beside you
              for that day
              when the heavens
              and the mountains
              shall move against me.
              In your great goodness,
              remember
              I was born
              of a sinner's womb.

ANGEL: We can do no more than wish for your good,
              for your welfare is our pleasure;
              not one soul would we wish to lose,
              but good is for you a lost treasure,
              for which you have no maps or chart,
              for you lived in days of blindness,
              locked in the darkness of your heart.

DEVIL: That must come as something of a shock

to one who has lived like you,
who has strutted through life like a peacock
prancing around in paradise.
Get on board and pick up an oar,
its time to pay my price.
By the way,
did you know
your wife slept with every last man
of the imperial guard?
I'll show you,
later.

Death returns.

DEATH: He looks as if he's had bad news.

DEVIL: I wouldn't like to be in his shoes,
what with eternal damnation...
and a loving wife who's slept with half the nation.

An Archbishop and Cardinal enter.

DEATH: You are in the presence of men of God,
veritable saints,
before whom you should fall on bended knee
and praise without restraint.
For how can you, a mere fallen angel,
condemned by the Holy Ghost
for spreading evil, sowing discontent,
amidst the heavenly host,
how dare you, a force for so much evil,
one who's wreaked such havoc,
stand unabashed before a cardinal
in his sumptuous cassock,
and of course the archbishop of Lisbon,
complete with mitre,
how can you stand before him and not quake,
such a born fighter
for good, one who strove for God's perfection?

DEVIL: The odour of sanctity,

the rich aroma of such saintly souls.
Yet worms work frantically,
feasting on your hearts, liquefying your brains,
the bodies, the form,
you dressed so exquisitely in fine robes,
are rotting aswarm
with God's tiny creatures of God's dark earth.
Turn to look this way
and you'll see your bodies in the ground
start to rot and to decay,
the ordeal by grass, the banquet of worms.
You look pained, Your Grace.
You traded in death, yet such images
are not to your taste?
You peddled hellfire like a whore sells flesh;
an empty sacrament.
You fuelled the panic and took their money!
You are excrement,
Your Grace.

ARCHBISHOP: We spoke of death so that souls would win life.

CARDINAL: We prepared the path.

DEVIL: You wielded the weight of holy mother church
                like a psychopath
                brandishes a sword or hoists a burning cross.
                The impoverished,
                the poor and the hopelessly abandoned
                could well have wished
                for words of comfort, for the love of Christ,
                but you let them feast
                on your poisoned words of fear and loathing,
                and with no money for their priest,
                you let them live and die in mortal terror.
                I admire your technique,
                your lucrative scheme for selling favours.
                And I like your cheek,
                in believing that heaven too is yours.

                LESSON

ARCHBISHOP: My spirit,
created by your hands,
is yours
and yours alone.
My days are cut short
and sadness
overflows within me.
I do not know
why you prepared my grave
thus.
I did not sin;
and I shall say to my decay:
you are my mother and my father,
whom I obey on earth.
The worm
I shall call
my sister and my friend.
My Lord,
why have you made
this enemy unto me?

RESPONSE

CARDINAL: I believe that my Redeemer lives
and that I shall see him.

DEVIL: It is only death that lives for ever.
Christ is dead in hell,
and it is in hell that you both shall burn.
Your soul's death knell
was sounded in your greed for sinners' alms.

ARCHBISHOP: *(to the Angel)* I lived my life in firmness and belief.
I upheld the law.

CARDINAL: I kept God's church powerful on earth.
You cannot ignore
what I have achieved in the name of Christ.

ANGEL: The name of Christ is love,
and there is no room for love in your hearts.

You raise your eyes to God above,
you bedeck yourselves with crook and mitre,
but yours are hearts of loathing.
You are not vicars of God, but bandits
in vicars' clothing.

CARDINAL: Such was my love for my fellow man –
such is my feeling –
that I stand beside this wretched sinner,
guilty of stealing
the money of the poor and of the church;
I urge him to confess
and you and I shall grant him absolution.

DEVIL: Such kindness, such largess!
You clearly walk on the side of angels...
such goodness is heaven sent.

ARCHBISHOP: You take the devil's word that I'm a thief?
Your theology is bent.
A cardinal should converse with angels.
not gossip with Satan.

CARDINAL: Your fear betrays your guilt; to remain silent
is to condone the sin.
Good Angel, announce me, I pray, to God.
I am ready to board;
and you, I am forced to abandon here.
You cannot defraud
the justice of God, his all-seeing eye.
Everything is seen.
I won't shake hands. Like those of unclean women,
who can tell where yours have been?

LESSON

ARCHBISHOP: I sinned every day
and did not repent.
I am heartily sorry.
Man born of woman
has the shortest of spans

for as the flower
that blooms and withers
so his soul is pursued.
As a shadow
we pass through life
and end our days in suffering
because through suffering
were we born.

CARDINAL: I think you've said enough, be on your way.
Your behaviour is tactless,
for it is time to turn our thoughts to God,
and your whining distracts us.

ANGEL: You have no response to his final prayer?

CARDINAL: His soul is surely dead,
and snatched beyond my jurisdiction.
What could I have said?

DEVIL: So the living will not speak to the dead,
nor goats to sheep?
But perhaps you curse your fallen friend to hell
because your own sin's so deep.

CARDINAL: I lived a life of exemplary faith,
a life fired by the hope
that on the duly appointed day...

DEVIL: ... they'd make you Pope.
Yes or no?

CARDINAL: The Pope was my confessor,
my spiritual guide.

DEVIL: The Pope was the object of your envy;
the goal of your pride
was to see him dead and well, well buried
with yourself empowered
to sit high and proud on the Holy See.

ANGEL: Your ambition towered
              over your faith, your hope and charity.

ARCHBISHOP: It was an open secret,
              that you burned to be the Holy Father.

DEVIL: Burn you will. So be it.

              LESSON

CARDINAL: I sinned
              in every waking thought,
              and knew not to repent.
              Have mercy on me!
              I was a Christian
              in my faith.
              Save me from suffering,
              oh eternal God.
              Save me from hell,
              where there is no redemption.
              Everlasting power,
              cure this evil of our times.
              I am lost
              and do not know
              where I must go.

              RESPONSE:

              Wounds of Christ,
              oars of this boat to heaven,
              speed me to heaven,
              let mercy be your sail.

DEVIL: You knew the inquisition
              of tortured desire, of obsessive schemes,
              of burning ambition.
              Your life and faith were martyred to your lust
              for naked power.

CARDINAL: May God strike me dead if...

DEVIL: He has.

CARDINAL: I was a tower
                   of Christian virtue and of piety.

DEVIL: You were infested
                   with the longing to have what you had not,
                   and you detested
                   everyone who possessed what you didn't,
                   who had what you lack,
                   and you had them burnt or their bodies broken
                   on the wheel or rack.
                   You did not see the beam in your own eye,
                   instead you blinded
                   the innocent, the poor and the frightened.

CARDINAL: I merely minded
                   God's law, applied it with all its rigour.
                   Shall I be condemned for that?

                   The sounds of an auto-da-fe begin to be heard.

DEVIL: The inquisition of youth.
                   The inquisition of women.
                   The inquisition of the happy.
                   The inquisition of all those
                   who aroused your envy,
                   who pricked your pride.
                   Remember,
                   one summer morning
                   your priests marched
                   one hundred
                   men, women and children,
                   into a Lisbon square
                   and stripped them
                   and burnt them alive.
                   To keep the plague at bay.
                   To appease your wrathful God,
                   you said.
                   Your auto da fe,
                   your act of faith,

you too are lost amongst the sheep.
Pray to your saviour
that this night he may keep
his bond that you have broken.
Pray that we may show you mercy
as a final token
of God's love for humankind.

Glorious Mary,
for the countless tears
you shed
in the shadow of the cross,
lift this shadow
from the our hearts,
release us from this suffering
which pierces
our souls
like nails.

Listen to the silence.
It is all around us, like a shroud.
Your prayers
your weeping
have not been answered.
It pains us
that such souls,
chosen above all others,
will go to the fires.
But in the errors
of your life
you did not remember him.
Cast off.

The sails are unfurled to reveal a painting of the crucifixion. All kneel.

Crucified shepherd,
will you remain deaf
to our prayers?
Why do you abandon your flock
this way?

was an act of hatred,
of a tortured soul
that knew only
how to torture,
of twisted desire
that knew only
how to twist
and break.
You burned
as I made you burn,
and you burned others
in your likeness.
Now you shall burn,
again.

Death enters, now accompanied by the Pope.

DEATH   *(to the Devil)* My reign is complete.
             You challenged
             my jurisdiction.
             Everything dies.
             Even the sea.

DEVIL: Vicarius Filii Dei.
             The Vicar of the Son of God.
             It has been written
             in the Book of the Apocalypse
             that by this sign
             shall you recognise him.
             The anti-christ.
             666.
             It is written in your name.
             Vicarius Filii Dei.
             Roman numerals
             read out your sin.
             Absolute and original.
             We are brothers
             you and I,
             and I welcome you
             to this dark abode.

POPE: Such trickery is beneath contempt.
I am the Holy Vicar of God
and this crude and vile attempt
to slander one in Peter's line
is worthy only of your kind.
Lucifer, return to the slime
whence you crawled, I command you.

DEVIL: And yet the number is written.

POPE: Satan I know you, I understand you,
but not because we are brothers.
I have looked into the human soul,
seen you and your infernal others
corrode the sacred temple of man.
I am the High Priest of man and God,
I know both you and your plan,
and I command you now: be gone.
I shall talk to you no more.

DEVIL: The head that wears the highest crown
should set the highest example.
From your holy throne you looked down
on those whose lives were written in pain and loss.
Your dignity set you apart,
your bore your majesty like a proud cross.
You were degraded by such pride;
you were corrupted by such power;
you rode high and mighty on the tide
of your majesty and glory.
And you never thought of the innocents
of body and soul that your church abused.

LESSON

POPE: Why bring man from the womb, Lord,
why raise him to your side?
Why make me your shepherd
and raise me on high?
It would have been better
not to be born,

not to have been,
not to have been seen
by the eyes of man,
only to be consumed
as wax in the fire.

RESPONSE

Have pity on me, Lor
For my life
has been written in si
What shall I do,
a miserable sinner?
Where shall I go,
a miserable sinner?
Oh infinite mercy,
have mercy on me.
Do not leave me to
for all eternity.
Command me
on this shore
in this dark night.
My soul
is thine
oh Lord.

DEVIL: My dead lords;
I have listened to y
and I rejoice in you
Life is but a falling
an ear of wheat the
You though you w
Dukes, Emperors,
Not one of you co
with egos the size
Yours was the ear
to God's heaven;
you brought hell t
For that you will

ANGEL: Good Shepherd,

POPE:

ANGEL:

POPE:

QUEEN:

My redeemer,
bring the boat to anchor,
divine creator,
human redeemer.

EMPEROR:

Captain
above all captains,
conqueror
of all conquerors.
Did you make us mortal
to suffer such evil?
Bring the boat to land.

CARDINAL:

Lord,
we are sorely afraid.
Put down their oars.
Lord,
we shall perish,
Command the gangway down.

DUKE:

Sweet lamb,
you suffered for us,
you were tormented
and died
in human form.
Do not keep us from
your promised lands.

ARCHBISHOP:

My messiah,
do not deny to us
the mercy that is in you.
Divine lamb,
doctor of our suffering,
our eternal fountain,
flesh of our flesh,
do not countenance
such suffering.

PRINCE:

Gentle son of God,
we are frightened,
we are blind.

We look upwards
and the sky is empty.
We strain to hear
and the sky is silent.
We are frightened.
We are frightened.

> *The Angels move farther from the shore. The*
> *crying of the souls rises and echoes like a song of*
> *lamentation. Their pain and suffering is plain.*
> *Christ the Redeemer appears and gives them the*
> *oars which are the wounds and dolours of*
> *crucifixion, and takes them with him. Only Death*
> *remains to contemplate the world.*